PRAISE FOR THE AUTHOR

"From great loss can come great learning. Navigating Alzheimer's – Survival Secrets of a Long Term Carer *can teach you not just how to survive dementia caring, but how to come out the other end a more resilient and resourceful person."*

Sharon Jurd, International Author and Speaker, Queensland, Australia.

"Carolyn's book is truly inspirational and her ability to push through tough times leaves the reader with lots of valuable life lessons on how to overcome adversity, still raise a family and hold down a high level career whilst caring for a loved one. This book has a message in it for everyone."

Darren Stephens, No. 1 Bestselling Author,

Millionaires & Billionaires Secrets Revealed, The 10 Day Turnaround – How to Transform Your Business Virtually Overnight and *The Success Principles.*

Navigating Alzheimer's *is easy, in fact enjoyable, to read. It tells the truth but retains that essential ingredient in life – a sense of humour. I believe it is particularly useful for Alzheimer's carers and may offer valuable insights for their medical professionals. This is a powerful story which will leave the reader wanting to know more.*

Dr Julie Coulson, Medical Practitioner, Tusmore, South Australia.

T0362961

"Really enjoyed reading your book. I think you are incredibly brave and kind sharing so many personal, physical and emotional moments from your family's journey. The depth of your compassion and love clearly was the catalyst of your drive and determination. [Anyone] reading the book will gain enormous comfort from your frank and honest conveyance of the many challenges you all faced and overcame.

The book provides the reader so much more than emotional strength and insight to fighting Alzheimer's. I think it guides individuals to stop, stand still and focus, to look at our values and to consider every challenge as an opportunity to produce something positive. For this I thank you.

I think your book will reach many people, and as above help them on their journey, whether caring for someone or just someone who needs a hug and encouragement to keep hope and strength."

David Yates, Property Manager, Adelaide, South Australia.

"Carolyn gets the right balance of humour and sensitivity just right as she shares her and Richard's love story alongside a disease which ultimately took her husband away from her. More importantly, Carolyn provides the reader with practical tips on supporting carers of those with Alzheimer's. Carers are the people who are often overlooked and Carolyn has now given them a voice. I can see this book assisting doctors with newly diagnosed patients as well as policy makers who need to make changes to the system to help patients and their carers in a more meaningful way. A wonderful insightful book."

Bee King, Manager, Adelaide, South Australia.

"Navigating Alzheimer's *provides a fresh, and very personal account of Alzheimer's disease. It is written with truth and honesty but also with a sense of humour, providing hope and inspiration for others. Despite the serious and difficult nature of this disease I found this book very readable and enjoyable. Carolyn has written openly about confronting issues including the veil of secrecy and fear associated with Alzheimer's disease and the sense of isolation that results for families affected by this disease. The insights in this book provide vital understanding, knowledge and direction for all of us who seek to provide support and assistance to family and friends dealing with Alzheimer's disease.*"

Dr Jane Hecker, MBBS (Hons), FRACP, FRCP (UK).

"*Wow… I have just finished your book. I couldn't put it down. Genuine, warm, sunny, poignant, challenging and just so beautifully written. Thank you for sharing your story.*"

Wendy O'Brien, Public Relations, Account Director, Adelaide.

HARDCORE RESILIENCE

7 Steps to Building Successful and Lasting Resilience in Your Business and Your Life

GLOBAL
PUBLISHING
GROUP

Global Publishing Group
Australia • New Zealand • Singapore • America • London

HARDCORE RESILIENCE

7 Steps to Building Successful and Lasting Resilience in Your Business and Your Life

CAROLYN CRANWELL LLB GDLP

International Author and Founder of the Global Psychometric Institute

First Edition 2023

National Library of Australia
Cataloguing-in-Publication entry:

1st ed.
ISBN: 978-1-925370-05-8 (pbk.)

 A catalogue record for this
book is available from the
National Library of Australia

Published by Global Publishing Group
PO Box 258, Banyo, QLD, 4014
Email admin@globalpublishinggroup.com.au

For further information about orders:
Phone: +61 7 3267 0747

I dedicate this book to my mother, Joy, for her unwavering courage, strength and wisdom.

TABLE OF CONTENTS

Acknowledgements   1
Foreword   3
Author's Note   7

Part I
What Is Resilience?   13
The Best Of Times ... The Worst Of Times   21

Part II
The Cranwell Resilience Ladder™   33
Step 1 - Acceptance   39
Step 2 - Self-Awareness   59
Step 3 - Purpose   75
Step 4 - Flexibility   91
Step 5 - Positive Mindset   107
Step 6 - Persistence   123
Step 7 - Staying Connected   139

Part III
The Cranwell-Cambridge Resilience Test™   155
Appendix I - Business Crisis Guidance Fast Track   164
Appendix II (a) - Crisis Plan Checklist - For Medium To Large Business 168
Appendix II (b) - Crisis Plan Template - For Medium To Large Business 171
Appendix III (a) - Crisis Plan Checklist - For Small Business Or Sole Proprietor 174
Appendix III (b) - Crisis Plan Template - For Small Business Or Sole Proprietor 177
About The Author   179
Recommended Resources   182
Notes   186

"The most fortunate of us all in our journey through life frequently meet with calamities and misfortunes which greatly afflict us. To fortify our minds against the attacks of these calamities and misfortunes should be one of the principal studies and endeavours of our lives."

Thomas Jefferson

ACKNOWLEDGEMENTS

This book could not have been written without inspiration and my readers will know that I have found this in many books, but none more than in the writings of Viktor Frankl.

I would like to also acknowledge the many amazing people from Australia and around the world whose stories have helped to illustrate this book about the steps we must take to achieve resilience. Reading about the measures they have taken to overcome their adversities and bringing their examples to you has been a continuing source of hope to me and a validation of the *Cranwell Resilience Ladder* ™.

Thank you to my family and friends for believing in me and to Terry for his continuous encouragement, support and humour.

Special thanks to Andrew Jefferis for his tireless work as my writing mentor and editor, to Darren Stephens and the team at Global Publishing for their direction and guidance, and to the Psychometrics Centre, University of Cambridge, for their expertise, professionalism and genuine collaboration in developing the *Cranwell-Cambridge Resilience Test* ™.

Carolyn Cranwell

FOREWORD

Helping people and businesses thrive has always appealed to me. I love the challenge of analysing a situation or a business, identifying the strengths and weaknesses and then making the tough decisions to turn the situation around.

That's how I developed an international reputation for being a "turnaround artist", someone who can quickly identify the potential to accelerate and maximise profits or someone who can lead individuals, businesses and large-scale organisations back from the brink of failure.

In my professional life, I have pioneered growth strategies in business leadership, personal development and spiritual alignment and I have been a featured speaker at business seminars and life acceleration workshops around the world.

I have shared the stage and program platforms with such business luminaries and thought-leaders as Jack Welch, Prime Minister Tony Blair, Stephen Covey, Seth Godin, Mark Thompson, Jay Abraham, Brendon Burchard, Jack Canfield, Dr. Kevin Hogan, Mark Victor Hansen, Joe Sugarman, John Assaraf, Darren J. Stephens, Chet Holmes and many others.

It was my good fortune to come across *Hardcore Resilience - 7 Steps to Building Successful and Lasting Resilience in Your Business and Your Life* through my long-term business colleague, successful publisher and entrepreneur Darren Stephens, with whom I wrote the bestseller *The Ten Day Turnaround – How To Transform Your Business Virtually Overnight...*

I was excited to read Carolyn Cranwell's refreshing concept of resilience. Frankly, I was delighted to see someone shake off the old notion that resilience is just a matter of 'bouncing back'. How can it be when sometimes the situation has changed so much it does not exist like it did before? No, I wholeheartedly agree with Carolyn. Hardcore sustainable resilience is required to enable you to continually move forward with confidence and success. This applies equally for individuals or for businesses.

Hardcore Resilience has been written with deep consideration, but also has Carolyn's light personal touch that makes it an easy read about a significant topic and is recommended for anyone – those challenged by change, facing adversity, seeking hope in the depth of despair, looking for courage but paralysed by fear, searching for stability in the era of uncertainty, or chasing sustainability and success now and in the future.

The author's and other well-known individuals' real-life experiences are what give *Hardcore Resilience* – authenticity, credibility, and applicability. We get to see and experience hardcore resilience through their eyes and learn practical strategies and tips that can put us back into the driver's seat again, in our businesses, in our relationships, and in our lives. The universal mystery surrounding resilience is de-mystified.

Hardcore Resilience - 7 Steps to Building Successful and Lasting Resilience in Your Business and Your Life challenges dated preconceptions that resilience is an attribute that cannot be taught and instills in us feelings of inspiration, hope, and personal empowerment. So, whether you are facing adversity or embarking on a major challenge in life, Carolyn's work will guide you to develop hardcore resilience for yourself, your business, your organisation, or your community.

I believe in a future where the morning mantra at home, conversations around the business water cooler or discussions in the corporate boardroom start with "So where are YOU on the Resilience Ladder today?" is inevitable.

Spike Humer

Business Growth Strategist, Performance Enhancement Expert

Las Vegas, Nevada, USA

AUTHOR'S NOTE

I am not a psychiatrist, psychologist or doctor. I am qualified as a lawyer, but most of my working career has been spent as a Senior Adviser to State Government on Counter-Terrorism Security and Emergency Management policy and advice for public transport systems.

My expertise in resilience has come from life. I have 18 years' experience as an Alzheimer's carer for my husband Richard who developed Younger Onset Alzheimer's when we had a young family and were both working hard in our careers.

I believe it is simple authentic true stories about lived experiences that enable most of us to understand and relate to complex concepts. I would love to tell you that resilience is easy but if that were true then everyone and every business could be as resilient as needed when disruption happens, but clearly this is not always the case.

For a long time, I have felt compelled to write this book. In mid-2019 it was weighing heavily on my mind.

After resigning from my job in December 2019, I flew to London to spend Christmas with my family. It was freezing in London, but back in Australia, where the summer heat had started early, all was quiet. But the peace was a brooding peace because of the sustained drought that had gripped much of the continent.

The explosion was immediate when it came.

Several weather patterns collided and lingered, there was searing heat, dry lightning, high winds, broken power lines, and the bushfire infernos raged taking 34 human lives and the lives of 480 million animals and destroying 5.4 million hectares of bushland (13 million acres – more than twice the size of Wales), 2,439 homes then came the Virus…

The case for writing and sharing my insights on resilience became even more compelling.

This book has been written for everyone, but especially with you in mind if:

- You fear change, uncertainty and disruption
- You feel stuck but don't know how to move forward
- In a crisis you "wish everything would just go back to normal"
- You are clinging to the past because you are afraid of failure
- Your business is struggling to survive in the Covid-19 economy
- Your employees are stressed and anxious about their future
- You are an employer looking for resilient people you can rely on in a crisis
- You are a recruiter looking for a new way to test for soft skills.

Thank you for taking the time to read this book. I hope you find the stories and insights helpful.

Carolyn Cranwell

PART I

NEED WORK

WHAT IS RESILIENCE?

The word "resilience" means different things to different people. There is currently no universally agreed definition of resilience.[1]

This book is based on my interpretation of resilience as a concept and my understanding gained through the lived experience of myself and others. To me, a resilient person is:

> *"... considered to be one who is capable of initiating and sustaining their own efforts and monitoring and disciplining their emotions when faced with challenges or difficult situations.*
>
> *They accept change and uncertainty as part of life even if they do not like the disruption or ambiguities that may arise from time to time. They are likely to be highly purposeful, positive, flexible and persistent. They do not fear failure, rather, they view mistakes or setbacks as valuable lessons to guide and inform future decisions.*
>
> *They are likely to possess a high level of self-awareness, self-belief, courage, stamina, competence and commitment, but are not afraid to seek support when faced with adverse situations in order to progress and move forwards."* Cranwell-Cambridge Resilience Test [TM]

More than just 'bouncing back'

Resilience is not just about the ability of an individual or business to 'bounce back' from a crisis. It involves so much more.

After a crisis there is no going back, only forwards. For example, millions of men, women and children died as a result of World War I and II, but the day the guns stopped firing, those who were left behind did not simply start to 'bounce back'. In many cases there was no one or no familiar place left. Returning 'home' was not an option. Many communities, families, friends, workers, cities, towns, villages, industries, infrastructure were either killed or destroyed. Despite such devastating loss, the survivors who possessed resilience skills moved forwards and started new and unfamiliar lives.

I believe resilience by its very nature is one of our most enduring human traits. It helps us carry on regardless of all odds; enables us to survive. Examples of resilience are all around us. There also seems to be an abundance of it in the animal and plant kingdoms and we don't ever seem to question the capacity of nature to recover and renew itself after terrifying setbacks – like fires and floods.

But to people, the setbacks often seem insurmountable.

Stories of failures or partial resilience-led recoveries are easy to come by. Every day we witness people turn up for work, stare down the running track, look up at the mountain to measure themselves against the odds. It frequently doesn't work. Obstacles are everywhere.

In this book we are interested in the toughest of recoveries, the 'hardcore' resilience examples and the features and skills that enable resilient businesses and people to stand out above the pack.

But what is Hardcore Resilience?

Hardcore Resilience is simply a term I developed to describe a unique type of resilience that is sustainable and successful. It takes the outdated concept of 'bouncing-back' one step further.

A business or person possessing Hardcore Resilience has not only mastered the art of practicing resilience but implemented it successfully in their business or personal lives and taken them to a higher level.

YES – Resilience can be taught!

Resilience is not something you can buy, borrow, or delegate. It must be learned and practised. As Jim Rohn says, "You can't hire someone else to do your push-ups for you,"[2] but the good news is that once mastered these skills can stay with you for life.

It is not uncommon to hear someone say words to the effect of, "Oh, I could never be resilient, because I haven't experienced a major trauma or life-changing event." However, resilience does not need to be born out of tragic circumstances. Anyone who has relentlessly pursued a dream will have developed some resilience along the way.

No one ever wakes up one day and says, "I'm going to win an Olympic Gold Medal" and then becomes an Olympian the very next day. A dream of that magnitude is going to take great effort on your behalf, but the goals, struggles and challenges you meet along the way and how you react to them is what will determine the outcome. Whether you are seeking an Olympic medal, a successful business or equipping yourself with sustainable resilience life skills, unless you stretch yourself there will be no opportunity for growth and development.

Everyone is Time Poor...

Everyone is time poor these days, so I have included a list of Take-Aways for Resilient Businesses and Individuals. In Part II, the *Cranwell Resilience Ladder™* you will find meaningful stories and powerful insights that will expand on these key points:

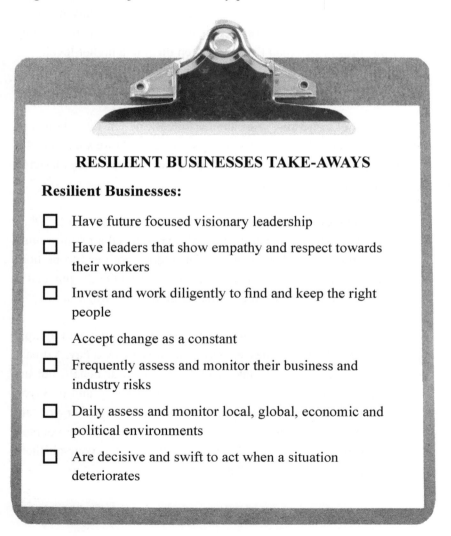

RESILIENT BUSINESSES TAKE-AWAYS

Resilient Businesses:

- ☐ Have future focused visionary leadership
- ☐ Have leaders that show empathy and respect towards their workers
- ☐ Invest and work diligently to find and keep the right people
- ☐ Accept change as a constant
- ☐ Frequently assess and monitor their business and industry risks
- ☐ Daily assess and monitor local, global, economic and political environments
- ☐ Are decisive and swift to act when a situation deteriorates

RESILIENT BUSINESSES TAKE-AWAYS

- ☐ Understand risk mitigation strengthens protection, productivity and continuity
- ☐ Prepare crisis strategies and plans for worst-case scenarios
- ☐ Constantly flex to embrace emerging trends and new markets
- ☐ Are externally focussed and have a customer-centric approach
- ☐ Treat their brand value and corporate reputation as sacrosanct
- ☐ Embrace change as an opportunity to grow and learn
- ☐ Always play to win, but are informed by failure, not daunted by it
- ☐ They are structured strategically to be at the forefront of innovation and creativity
- ☐ Always adhere to their core values creating a safe and positive environment for employees
- ☐ Listen to their staff and clients
- ☐ Foster and appreciate staff and client loyalty
- ☐ Often have solutions before rival businesses have realised the problem

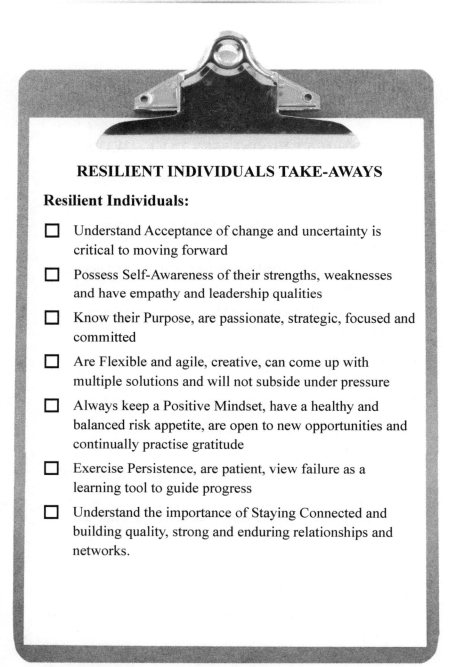

RESILIENT INDIVIDUALS TAKE-AWAYS

Resilient Individuals:

- ☐ Understand Acceptance of change and uncertainty is critical to moving forward

- ☐ Possess Self-Awareness of their strengths, weaknesses and have empathy and leadership qualities

- ☐ Know their Purpose, are passionate, strategic, focused and committed

- ☐ Are Flexible and agile, creative, can come up with multiple solutions and will not subside under pressure

- ☐ Always keep a Positive Mindset, have a healthy and balanced risk appetite, are open to new opportunities and continually practise gratitude

- ☐ Exercise Persistence, are patient, view failure as a learning tool to guide progress

- ☐ Understand the importance of Staying Connected and building quality, strong and enduring relationships and networks.

THE BEST OF TIMES…
THE WORST OF TIMES

> **❝**It was the best of times, it was the worst of times, it was the age of wisdom, it was the age of foolishness, it was the epoch of belief, it was the epoch of incredulity, it was the season of darkness, it was the spring of hope, it was the winter of despair.**❞**
> **Charles Dickens[3]**

In *A Tale of Two Cities*, Charles Dickens writes of the economic and political unrest that led to the American and French Revolutions. Dickens describes his world as a time when humanity was balancing on the precipice of turmoil, but desperately hoping for a better future.

Does this situation sound familiar? Of course it does, but in contrast to Dickensian times, the uncertainty and devastation in the world today is exponentially scaled up, and the angst, fear and uncertainty is spread globally.

As readers of the Global Risks Report (January 2021, 16th Edition) published by the World Economic Forum will acknowledge, if ever there was a case to build resilience worldwide – now is the time.

No matter what direction we look, locally, nationally or globally, a disaster could strike at any time and there is no shortage of impending crises. These circumstances may include the threat of further pandemics, cyberattacks, war, terrorism, the digital divide, climate change, international trade sanctions, fuel shortages, supply chain failure, environmental disasters, mass unemployment and lost opportunities for young people, and many more. Our personal lives can be just as complex.

"Learning and innovation go hand in hand. The arrogance of success is to think that what you did yesterday will be sufficient for tomorrow."
C. William Pollard[4]

The 'Crisis du Jour'

Not surprisingly, change and uncertainty are something most of us seek to avoid, but in 2022 the saying 'comfort zone' has almost become a misnomer.

But how do human beings and businesses cope and survive in a rapidly changing and uncertain environment? Is there a magic formula? No, but living through these conditions is certainly a life skill and one that can only improve with practice. Being resilient, being your authentic self, knowing your strengths and weaknesses, your core values, your purpose and how to focus on it is critical in these times of global upheaval. Although we live in an era of outsourcing, no one can do this for you. Admittedly the stakes for overcoming the fear of change and uncertainty are high but it's entirely up to you. You will always have a choice…

"I was set free because my greatest fear had already been realised, and I was still alive, and I still had a daughter whom I adored, and I had an old typewriter and a big idea. And so rock bottom became the solid foundation on which I rebuilt my life."
J.K. Rowling[5]

As to my own experience, for many years I had so much uncertainty in my daily life that I labelled these traumatic events the 'Crisis du Jour'. Giving these phenomena a name empowered me. Although only a concept in my imagination, it became something powerful, almost 'tangible'. I turned the tables and recast my uncertainty into my certainty. We formed an 'odd alliance', but the situation had improved. I still felt the fear, but the feelings started to become manageable. I then went one step further and secretly declared myself an 'Expert' in handling the Crisis du Jour and then did my level best to live up to the reputation I had so ambitiously given myself. I still had no control over the events that transpired but through this newly acquired covert identity I was able to cope better and coexist with uncertainty and, with practice, my learned tolerance and reactions soothed me and they gradually became bearable.

What Silicone Valley afficionados may overlook telling you...

Artificial intelligence is becoming increasingly common in large businesses such as online platforms (e.g., social networks or search engines, telecommunications, banking and financial services and retail sales etc.) and it's no secret that Covid-19 has accelerated digital uptake, but human nature has not progressed at a corresponding rate. Businesses and industries the world over are now challenged to find a way for the workforce to coexist with them as they adapt and digitally transform.

While the potential economic benefits of speed, upscaling, increased capability and productivity appear clear, I suggest the integration and interaction between technology and the human race is far from straightforward. Not all employees have the same risk appetite, skill set or depth of resilience for rapidly escalating change. Those without personal resilience skills may struggle with a loss of certainty, identity, and feelings of fear, anxiety and displacement.

Employers expect and need to be able to rely on their workforce to keep the business operating in times of change and when emergencies or a crisis occurs. Promoting those with resilience skills to leadership positions and providing resilience skills training is one way to reinforce business capabilities. A strategic resilient leadership team working on the business and a purpose-driven dedicated workforce working in the business can act as a buffer against substantial external forces, whatever they may be. I believe the secret to a resilient business lies in its people and their level of resilience.

COVID-19 has changed the world forever...

Early in my State Government career as a Senior Adviser in Counter-Terrorism Security and Emergency Management for public transport systems, I was fortunate to participate in a national epidemic exercise in response to a hypothetical outbreak of the Avian Flu, H5N1. It was an amazing opportunity to experience the level of 'behind the scenes' organisation and coordination required to mount a nationwide government response, maintain essential services and resume full business services when safe to do so.

However, when real life intervened and the outbreak of Avian Flu and later the Ebola Virus happened internationally, many Australians found the potential consequences of these outbreaks hard to get their heads around. Not surprisingly they appreciated the seriousness of such events, but they were not something they could easily relate to or imagine happening on home soil. Mostly our experience was based on the poliomyelitis or infantile paralysis (Polio) epidemics that had occurred in Australia in the late 1930s, early 1940s and 1950s. Since that time generations of Australians have grown up with a sense of safety and security derived from the success of the mass immunisation program and Australia's isolation from the rest of the world.

When the World Health Organisation finally declared a Covid-19 pandemic on March 11, 2020, the way most people ran their businesses and their lives was disrupted beyond their imagination. For many this phenomenon created a limbo-like state wedging them between the past and their strange new unwelcome reality.

In the early days after the declaration, I frequently observed morning talk show hosts and social media posts lamenting the state the world was in and longing for the time "when life gets back to normal" as if the pandemic had a finite recovery time.

Someone with strong sustainable resilience will be able to quickly sense the absence of elasticity in this situation. They will recognise bouncing back is not an option. 'Back' as a destination does not exist any longer, except in their memory and in history. They will accept the fact that yesterday is where it belongs – in the past. They will also accept that the only way out of a crisis is continually moving forwards.

"It's no use going back to yesterday because I was a different person then."
Lewis Carroll, Alice's Adventures in Wonderland[6]

I genuinely understand how difficult it is to let go of all that is familiar and valued when the future is so unclear and uncertain, but in a pandemic, waiting for yesterday to return is like waiting for a genie to voluntarily return to its bottle. It's not going to happen and forever is a long time to be waiting in vain… History has taught us the tragic consequences of disruptive events such as World War I, the Spanish Flu and World War II can continue to impact upon lives and businesses for many years and in some cases even decades.

The most precious business resource of all…

While there is a definite focus on resilience for business, this book concentrates on how to build strong sustainable successful resilience in the most precious business resource of all i.e., the people working in the business.

The solution to acquiring the skills to adapt, survive and thrive through traumatic universal changes and uncertainty is the core subject of this book. Hardcore Resilience – *7 Steps to Lasting Success in Your Business and in Your Life* clarifies and simplifies the key components and resilience skills necessary to strengthen, future-proof, and transform our businesses, work and personal lives. These skills are like the steps on a ladder and although they may be interchangeable you cannot afford to miss any. Read on!

Author's Note: For those seeking more information about resilient businesses and business crisis management planning and plans please turn to the Appendices.

THE SPANISH FLU

During 1918-20 the Type A H1N1 virus caught a world distracted by World War I completely by surprise. Called the Spanish Flu because Spain, unlike the US and most of Europe, did not censor the news and seek to quell any panic and appear unpatriotic during the war. It arose perhaps in Fort Riley, Kansas, amongst the troops, perhaps in Europe or Asia. Record keeping was poor and the first wave was mild. By the Autumn of 1919 it re-emerged and this time it was much more deadly, killing often in two days with no antidotes. Massive doses of aspirin, that some doctors trialled, proved as lethal as the flu itself. Some records say 17 million dead, others 50, with estimates as high as 100 million. It infected 500 million with the world population three times that number.

We can see some parallels with the Covid-19 crisis.

Type A H1N1 had at first been mistaken for a mild infection and underestimated. Borders could not be blocked because so many soldiers were returning home from the war and many were infected and undernourished, suffered poor hygiene and sanitation and a lack of medical staff – all caused by the war effort that affected many countries and communities.

Businesses were shuttered in many cities and a lot were closed down. Mail was disrupted and lack of farm workers for the harvest lead to food shortages. New York City ordered staggered shifts for workers to avoid subway overcrowding. People were encouraged to wear masks. Cities that locked down meeting places more rigorously than others slowed the infection rate dramatically.

The silver lining with this particular virus was that if you recovered from the virus you developed immunity. Although the world community was spared further tragedy when the virus burned itself out early in 1920, there is evidence that people had been weakened by the infection and that many businesses struggled all the way to the Great Depression.

Due to the war effort unemployment in the US in 1918 was 1.4% but the post-war recession increased it to 11.7%. Recovery came with farm tariffs, and businesses and government embracing new technology by way of rubber, steel and the widespread use of electricity. By 1923 unemployment was down to 4%. The US seemed to be leaving trouble behind as it bounced forward.[7]

PART II

The Resilience Ladder

PERSISTENCE

POSITIVE MINDSET

FLEXIBILITY

STAYING CONNECTED

PURPOSE

SELF AWARENESS

ACCEPTANCE

THE CRANWELL
RESILIENCE LADDER™

Time is of the essence

There has never been a better time than now to develop Hardcore Resilience skills.

Back-to-back years of stress and emotional hardship followed by much reflection led me to develop a new concept named the **Cranwell Resilience Ladder™** (the 'Resilience Ladder') which sets out and simplifies the key principles for developing strong, sustainable, successful resilience.

There are seven steps on the *Resilience Ladder*:

1. Acceptance

2. Self-Awareness

3. Purpose

4. Flexibility

5. Positive Mindset

6. Persistence

7. Staying Connected

For clarity I have dedicated a chapter to each step and used stories and quotes to illustrate and differentiate each step's unique criteria and characteristics.

How did I develop this concept?

I reflected on long periods of particularly challenging and tough times in my life and how I approached, managed and survived them. A consistent pattern emerged and this pattern is reflected in the steps of the Resilience Ladder today.

How do you navigate the Resilience Ladder?

Imagine if you were facing a life-changing business or personal crisis and to survive you were advised to 'snap out of it' and transform yourself immediately, becoming proficient in all areas of resilience simultaneously.

Understandably it would just be too much for most people.

But we all need to start somewhere. So, start at Step 1 – Acceptance, and work your way upwards. The 'steps' will provide you with a manageable 'bite-size' approach to give confidence as you progress.

Do you have to start at Step 1 – Acceptance, or can I jump a few steps ahead and start further up the Ladder?

No jumping! (At least not in the beginning).

Step 1 – Acceptance is absolutely critical to your success on the Resilience Ladder. It is imperative to start your resilience journey with Acceptance and master that step first because without full acceptance of change or adversity your business or personal recovery will be unbelievably frustrating, grossly ineffective and seriously compromised. Skipping the Acceptance step would be like building a house without solid stable foundations, you would be setting yourself up for certain failure.

Once you have cleared Acceptance, it is best to follow the steps in ascending order before you move on to the next one.

However, while there is a logical flow to ascending the Resilience Ladder in chronological order you may find your individual circumstances dictate a need to leapfrog or transcend a combination of steps simultaneously, not necessarily strictly in the prescribed order. Don't be alarmed. This is alright. Everyone's abilities and circumstances are different. The Resilience Ladder is indeed a framework but it is not lacking in flexibility!

For instance, you might find in the process of working towards and achieving your Purpose (Step 3) or questioning your outlook on business and life in Positive Mindset (Step 5), that you find yourself sliding backwards considering your strengths and weaknesses i.e., in Self-Awareness (Step 2).

If this happens, think of the Resilience Ladder as more of a designated track and you need to stay within the rails. At different times you may need to move up and down the Resilience Ladder but if you stay within the vertical lines and don't get distracted and venture off sideways it is much easier to refocus and recommence the climb.

On another day you might feel so overwhelmed by your situation that you want to quit and admit defeat, but – NO, don't stop. Just keep going… This Resilience Ladder is symbolic of your life trajectory. Returning your Resilience Ladder to the hardware store is not an option!

So pause, take a moment and reflect back in time as far as you need to go till you reach a point in your life when your circumstances were better and what that felt like. Then think about why you are doing this now and what you want to achieve – i.e., your Purpose (Step 3).

Then remind yourself about the things in your life you are grateful for i.e., in Positive Mindset (Step 5) and in doing so you may find the extra courage and strength you need to keep going.

In Persistence (Step 6), remember that you have choices and you are the one in control. You are a survivor, not a victim. Quitting on yourself is a luxury you cannot afford… ever.

It's simply a matter of working the steps and then making the steps work for you

Still feeling daunted? If in doubt you may need to fast track the lower steps to reach Step 7 – Staying Connected, in order to get support and reassurance from a mentor, work colleague, family member or friend. Granted, asking for help is not always easy but it can certainly lighten your 'load'. People are often very willing to help but sometimes refrain because they don't know what to do. Often it is tempting to think "Oh, it's quicker and easier if I do everything myself" and not involve others. I know this for a fact. In the past I have fallen for this trap more than once myself. It's not just the asking for help hurdle to overcome here. There is an element of Acceptance to be recognised and acknowledged i.e., Accepting the fact that the only way forward may require asking for help from others, but don't be afraid to blow the bugle and summon the cavalry. Help might be closer than you think.

A lack of supportive positive connections can isolate us and drag us down while positive connections can give us strength and fortitude to survive and succeed. Although Staying Connected is the final 'step' for purposes of completing the Resilience Ladder, our ongoing ability to stay connected may also resemble a reinforcing web that strengthens and binds together our continuous progress.

As you ascend the Resilience Ladder, don't be afraid to look back and review the steps you have taken and revisit them as many times as you feel necessary. Looking back while in contemplation of the way ahead is not failure.

Any perspective gained will only help enhance your understanding of what constitutes authentic resilient behaviour and this in turn will increase your ability to sustain these practices successfully over the long term.

Now we will take a close look at each step on the Resilience Ladder.

So where are you on the Resilience Ladder today?

STEP 1 - ACCEPTANCE

THE CRANWELL RESILIENCE LADDER ™ - STEP 1

"Authentic unfiltered acceptance is both the keystone and hallmark of a resilient person.**"**
Carolyn Cranwell

Resilient people understand that **acceptance** is critical to moving forward and that is the theme as we take our first steps upon the Ladder…

Total Acceptance

Total Acceptance of a crisis facilitates the understanding that one must accept change exactly as the situation has manifested itself because some situations are totally beyond our control. The act of denial cannot orchestrate a reversal of fortune or create momentum. Only unfiltered acceptance of change can liberate you from stagnation and unfortunately there are no shortcuts or easy ways out to finding acceptance. Inward reflection is necessary to get external action.

Face life head on

Turning towards life's storms and facing them head on can be mentally, physically, emotionally and financially confronting and draining. However, left unfettered undesirable obstacles or challenges are liable to escalate exponentially in your imagination creating far greater stress and worry than if they had been dealt with swiftly and decisively from the beginning.

Resilient people understand that acceptance does not mean you have to like the situation or be happy about it before you accept it

Resilient people are characteristically quick to accept changes no matter what the circumstances, but remember, resilient people are not superhuman. When tragedy strikes them, they may feel shocked, saddened, scared, disappointed, disillusioned, confused, angry or even devastated. They may distinctly dislike or even passionately hate the chaos or grief they are experiencing, but they realise denying the existence of such change is futile and will not improve or alter their situation.

Resilient people understand that denial can be dangerous

They recognise that a change-resistant attitude will always hold them back from healing, innovating, finding solutions and remedies (where possible), progressing and ultimately moving forward. In other words, they understand that without acceptance of their new situation (as painful as that may be) they are essentially trapped.

Viktor Frankl, the Austrian psychiatrist who survived inhumane conditions in Auschwitz and other Nazi concentration camps, chose to survive to be reunited with his beloved wife and to share his message of hope and meaning with the world. Frankl believed that no matter how grave the circumstances, the freedom to choose how we respond to a situation is something that is entirely within our own control:

> **"**Even though conditions such as lack of sleep, insufficient food and various mental stresses may suggest that the inmates were bound to react in certain ways, in the final analysis it became clear that the sort of person the prisoner became was the result of an inner decision and not the result of camp influences alone.**"** [8]

Resilient people refuse to vacate the driver's seat in their own lives

They recognise choices still exist even when there appear to be none. Frankl wrote in *Man's Search for Meaning*:

> **"**Forces beyond control can take away everything you possess except one thing, your freedom to choose how you will respond to the situation. You cannot control what happens in life, but you can always control what you will feel and do about what happens to you.**"** [9]

Though there was no semblance of the life he once owned, Viktor Frankl still dictated life on his terms and you can too.

So how does one accept a life-changing crisis, live for years with uncertainty or survive a devastating tragedy?

Well, to simplify and illustrate this point I refer to an old riddle:

Question: How do you eat an elephant?

Answer: One bite at a time.

First of all, you would have to accept there is an elephant in the room in the first place, wouldn't you? Of course, because you can't eat an invisible elephant. You start with the first bite and then you just keep chewing.

It is how quickly we accept and adapt to the presence of the 'elephant' that any progress moving forward can be made. Pretending the elephant is invisible is like being knee deep in mud. You aren't going anywhere fast and the longer the denial persists the deeper you become bogged.

DYLAN ALCOTT OAM

No stranger to Australians, he was presented with the Medal of the Order of Australia (OAM) in 2009 for service to sport as a Gold Medallist in wheelchair basketball at the Beijing 2008 Paralympic Games. A Silver Medal followed in London in 2012.

More honours came when he was named Australian Paralympian of the Year after winning double Gold Medals in the Paralympics Men's Singles and Doubles Tennis at the 2016 Olympic Games in Rio de Janeiro.

As if that wasn't enough, 2021 turned into Dylan's golden year! His victories included Grand Slam Quad Singles (Australian Open, French Open and Wimbledon) and the Quad Doubles (Australian Open) and then in September he topped it off with more gold in the Tokyo Paralympics Quad Singles becoming the only man to win all four major events in the same year. What a star! Recognition of these outstanding achievements followed in 2022 when he was awarded the Victorian State Representative of the Year, Australian of the Year and he was made an Officer of the Order of Australia for "distinguished service to paralympic sport, particularly to tennis, and as a role model for people with disability and to the community through a range of organisations."

Dylan not only excels in wheelchair basketball and wheelchair tennis, but he is also regarded as a charismatic, entertaining radio and TV personality and DJ and an articulate advocate for disability.

At birth a tumour was removed from his spinal cord leaving him without lower body movement. As a teenager Dylan was socially confident but he soon realised that he would be treated at a disadvantage unless he took matters into his own hands. One of his own memories' recounts being excluded from a friend's party ('the invitation that never arrived'). He decided nevertheless to turn up. His friend apologised that he had been trying to save Dylan from embarrassment because of the poor wheelchair access in his house where the party was held. Dylan says of himself that he was a 'hot' guest that night, becoming 'the life of the party' and was even "kissed by girls"![10]

As an example of Acceptance, we can say that Dylan Alcott is aware of his own choices and has always chosen not to be a victim, but to insist that he is treated equally and without pity. He does not dither or hesitate and is always emphatic and immediate in his attitude to disability and stigmatised treatment. For example, when speaking to disabled young people, he has said: *"The biggest thing is that for every one thing you can't do, there are 10,000 others you can. For every one idiot to give you a hard time, there are 10,000 others worth your time."*[11] He is very much an advocate for us all to take on challenges, whether we are able-bodied or disabled. For Dylan there is no difference.

This humble Melbourne superstar is not just a shining example to wheelchair athletes. Despite physical disability his tenacity and the way he triumphs through living his life full on is nothing short of a masterclass for us all.

Partial acceptance is not enough

The passage below from Diane Coutu further illustrates the importance of completely unfiltered acceptance and how important this can be to one's survival:

> A common belief about resilience is that it stems from an optimistic nature. That's true but only as long as such optimism doesn't distort your sense of reality. In extremely adverse situations, rose-coloured thinking can actually spell disaster. This point was made poignantly clear to me by management researcher and writer Jim Collins, who happened upon this concept while researching *Good to Great*, his book on how companies transform themselves out of mediocrity. Collins had a hunch (an exactly wrong hunch) that resilient companies were filled with optimistic people. He tried out that idea on Admiral Jim Stockdale, who was held prisoner and tortured by the Vietcong for eight years. Collins recalls: "I asked Stockdale: 'Who didn't make it out of the camps?' And he said, 'Oh, that's easy. It was the optimists. They were the ones who said we were going to be out by Christmas. And then they said we'd be out by Easter and then out by Fourth of July and out by Thanksgiving, and then it was Christmas again.' Then Stockdale turned to me and said, 'You know, I think they all died of broken hearts.'"[12]

The prisoners of war who Admiral Stockdale spoke about had varying levels of resilience, but clearly those who accepted and faced the total reality of their situation and the uncertainty of the war were the ones who endured captivity. From the prisoners' story we learn that total, not partial acceptance of one's new reality can be absolutely critical to survival.

SHANE FITZSIMMONS

Shane Fitzsimmons shot to national fame in Australia when his face and calm, authoritative voice came onto our TV screens daily during the New South Wales (NSW) Bushfires of 2019–20. Political leaders often lead the press conferences in times of emergency but this time it was mainly Commissioner Fitzsimmons heading the proceedings.

On one day there were 170 fires burning in the region and 17 of them were at emergency alert level.

Shane Fitzsimmons had been a fire fighter for 35 years, he had recovered from a 'wild' childhood by joining the Fire Service, he had lost his father in a truck rollover while fighting a fire, he married Lisa from a fire-fighting family, but more than that he had faced the 'wall of flames' many times himself and he knew about the fatigue, the panic, the personal loss and the sheer heat that his 72,000 NSW volunteer fire fighters had to bear.[13]

Where does his Resilience come from? Does it come from his teachers telling him he would land in gaol if he *"kept that up"* as a teenager? Does it come from the conflict of loving his dad but having to protect his mum when his dad George, would get drunk and beat her? Or the message in 1994, *"Sorry mate, your dad didn't make it."* Certainly, Shane's Acceptance would have been helped by the family of his girlfriend Lisa (now his wife of many years), who took him in and showed him what a functional family looked like and helped direct him towards the thing he was really good at: facing the crisis of a bushfire and choosing to be a survivor.[14]

Shane Fitzsimmons was named NSW Australian of the Year 2020 and appointed the inaugural Head of Resilience NSW, the State Government disaster agency. Late in the Australian Summer of 2020–21 he was back leading his State during more devastation caused by the heavy rain. It is called the 1 in 100-year flood and while announcing rescue and recovery measures, his acceptance and empathy were evident when he asked people to *"not give up on hope."*[15] Further recognition and honours followed when Shane was appointed an Officer of the Order of Australia in the 2022 Australia Day Honours for "distinguished service to the community through leadership roles within fire and emergency response organisations."

The more I live the more I realise very few people get through life unscathed. Health, financial or relationship issues can catch up with all of us at any time. Without the help of a crystal ball we just don't know how, when or where.

But there was a time in my life when fortune favoured me and I had everything – everything in life that really mattered and I had all of it, all at the same time. How many people do you know that can say that? I'm not sharing this with you to boast or to make you feel bad but to provide some context to my personal story and how I learnt about the importance of acceptance.

I had a loving husband, two beautiful children, we all enjoyed good health, family and friends, a home of our own. We had fulfilling employment, good food, access to medical services when necessary and we lived in a peaceful and free country. We were undeniably happy and content, but this 'Camelot-like' existence was so finely balanced, it only took one domino tile to fall before the whole line of tiles that symbolised our lives, began to fall.

Changes that can impact on our personal lives and/or business are so unpredictable and may be frequent throughout our lifetimes. While some of these changes may be anticipated and welcomed, others may be sudden and brutal.

KELLOGG AND THE GREAT DEPRESSION

After the euphoria of the end of the Great War society was ebullient and the stock market gradually became bullish. New industries and technologies flowed out of the war effort and the major cities embraced new wealth and social freedoms. For many their inhibitions were down. We have all heard of the Roaring Twenties. As the new confidence led to many people flocking to the big cities to make their fortunes all was not well in the agricultural sector, particularly in the US. Overproduction in agriculture often caused by new farming techniques left severe financial pressure. There was very high debt, very low wages and the existence of very large bank loans. Britain and Germany also owed huge sums to the US from the war.

People wanted to believe that the stock market would sustain the fever pitch of speculation and go on rising for ever and ever. They were cautioned by the Federal Reserve on March 25, 1929, and a small crash followed. The Market in Wall Street was like a dramatic rollercoaster for the next few months. In London the Stock Exchange crashed when prominent investors were jailed for fraud. Confidence plummeted on both sides of the Atlantic until in New York on Black Thursday (24th) and Black Monday (28th), when markets began to slide. Slide led to panic. There was a run on the banks with fever-pitched selling.

The effects were felt everywhere. The prosperity that surrounded the cities was suddenly found to be paper thin. What followed was the Great Depression: with steep declines in industrial production, rapid price deflation, mass unemployment, banking panic, extreme poverty and high levels of homelessness. The US faced severe drought and international trade (not helped by new protectionist trade laws) plummeted. Unemployment had risen between 23% and 33% globally.[16]

At Kellogg the approach was different. This company had always been ahead of the game with innovations and inventions, but when the depression hit, they doubled their advertising budget, going heavily into radio, pushed a new product, Rice Krispies (sold in Australia as Rice Bubbles) and took on more staff. Their main competitor, Post, did the opposite and never caught up the difference in prosperity. Because of the crippling rate of unemployment Kellogg kept their staff on, encouraging part-time hours if it meant they could spread the work. (They kept this practice going until after the Second World War.) By 1933 profits had risen 30% and Kellogg have stayed world leaders in their industry ever since.

According to the *New Yorker*, most businesses however still follow the model of Post and contract staff until times are better: "*In 1927 the economist Roland Vaile found that firms that kept advertising spending stable, or increased it during the recession of 1921–22 saw their sales hold up significantly better than those which didn't.*"[17] This result has continued to play out in numerous recessions or economic contractions since then.

We can see that Kellogg responded rapidly, accepted the new situation, turned from potential victim to survivor and consciously moved on despite the risk. Their actions to increase shifts while asking existing employees to go part-time so that they could give work to more staff was ultimately an act of empathy (which I discuss in the next chapter). This was no doubt out of concern for the citizens of Battle Ridge, but the company was quick to accept that with extreme poverty all around them, they could neither function nor sell their products.

When storm clouds caught up with me...

"A sticky plaque-like 'fog' had settled on parts of Richard's brain and it was causing havoc with his communication, thinking and memory systems.**"**
Carolyn Cranwell, Navigating Alzheimer's – Survival Secrets of a Long Term Carer

Early 2003, turned out to be a significant time for my family. It was the time when the reality of the vulnerability and frailty of the life we cherished, surreptitiously caught up with us and held us in a vicelike grip. Everything that we loved and that was familiar got turned completely upside down. The shock of the change in our lives alone hit us massively but worse, all certainty disappeared.

For 18 years out of our 32-year marriage, my husband Richard had younger onset Alzheimer's Disease Alzheimer's is a 'life sentence' in the true meaning of the words, far exceeding most courts' sentencing powers or jurisdiction. Why this happened to such a young healthy man, no one knows. It just did. There was no family history of the disease or any identifiable lifestyle causes. Even so, I do not believe we were singled out by some cosmic force or divine spirit. No one was to blame. Sometimes life just happens. Like Alan Saunders' words later used by John Lennon: *"Life is what happens to you while you're busy making other plans."*[18]

I won't insult you by pretending any of this was easy. It was tough when we got the diagnosis. It was tough watching Richard deteriorate into a shadow of his former self and it was tough watching him day after day, year after year suffering and slowly dying and not being able to do a single solitary thing to prevent this outcome.

You know you have a real problem when all the money in the world could not have altered the outcome

Sitting in the doctor's office and confronted with devastating test results and a terminal prognosis of up to 20 years was about as surreal as it gets, but all the medical evidence was there and it was clear and unequivocal. Richard's struggles for the last few years at home and at work only reinforced the 'news' of the diagnosis. Alzheimer's had

Richard undeniably in checkmate. Fear and grief were quick to set in for all of us.

However, sooner rather than later, I realised acceptance was the only way through what was to come. I had sat in the doctor's office with Richard for every visit and I had seen all the test results. Accepting such a life-changing event may initially seem such a counterintuitive thing to do, but Richard and our family were depending on me to lead the way forward.

It all comes down to choices

It is often said that there are no options in a situation like this, but I do not believe that is true. There was a clear choice to be made. Were we going to be victims or survivors? How would it have helped Richard if we had taken on the mantle of victims? What good would that have done for him or for the children?

❝In reality, survival just comes down to a simple straightforward decision. A conscious act of will might be another way to describe it but whatever you want to call it, it is just a choice… and I chose to survive right from the beginning. I believe this is what kept me strong and what kept us all going.❞
Carolyn Cranwell, Navigating Alzheimer's – Survival Secrets of a Long-Term Carer

---

Our new reality wasn't like the Olympics when you have had years of training and a coach guiding your every move. At first it felt like a toxic cocktail of raw fear and emotional pain on a level I had never experienced before. Slowly I began to thaw out from the initial shock. After a few weeks I realised there was absolutely no alternative. The only thing that was capable of change was me. Gradually I managed to readjust my primal 'fear and flight' reflex into a 'fear and fight' attitude and so we bunkered down and dug our heels in for the long haul.

Set your own terms

If we had to accept that Alzheimer's had entered our lives it was going to be on our terms, so I chose to make Alzheimer's fit in with us, at least in the decade before Richard left the family home and entered fulltime care. Now that might sound like a ridiculous thing to say but the only alternative was to surrender completely to this disease and let it rule all our lives. I decided that simply wasn't an option. It was traumatic enough to know that Alzheimer's would eventually take Richard's life, without allowing the disease to completely sabotage all our lives as well in the process. Seeing the situation through his eyes I knew it is the last thing he would have wanted too.

Continual adjustments

In the early years Richard was still able to function moderately well, albeit with some assistance. This enabled us to maintain some semblance of family life. We coped by making a series of continual adjustments to all our routines when and where necessary. This appearance of normality minimised Richard's anxiety and restored some much-needed confidence for him and for the family.

Accepting continual change

It was amazing how quickly we adapted our behaviour to accept continual change. Uncertainty and apprehension just became a way of life. However, I can assure you, living under constant and considerable stress isn't always pretty, but if you ever find yourself in an emotional whirlpool like we did, remember survival mode requires neither elegance nor grace to be successful. No one is going to die if their shirt is hung out to drip dry rather than be ironed or if their evening meal is less Cordon Bleu silver service and more 'Cordon Meatloaf'.

My level of acceptance wasn't an exact science by any means and there were plenty of days when try as I would, I felt like I was walking backwards in quicksand but still we accepted our circumstances and persisted. It was clear our young family didn't fit in with the normal profile of a family supporting a member with Alzheimer's, but at least by accepting Alzheimer's as part of our way of life, we managed to maintain the comfort of our own home and familiar surroundings and familiar school and work routines and environment. At a time of rapid and escalating change it was a great emotional and mental comfort to maintain some sense of continuity, belonging and security which ultimately added to the way our family navigated Alzheimer's.

PHAN THI KIM PHUC

Vietnam was the war of journalists and photojournalists. They brought it into our living rooms in the sixties and seventies every evening. There was no avoiding it. Once Australia had troops in combat areas it was no longer 'interesting'. It had a perilous edge… and it was divisive. Generations argued about it, students marched and clashes with the police became violent.

It is little wonder that Nick Ut's photo taken June 8, 1972, galvanised such protest around the world: A little nine-year old South Vietnamese girl mistakenly bombed with napalm by her own country's troops, running down the street horrifically burned… she later recalled she was yelling, *Nóng quá, nóng quá ("Too hot, too hot")*. The photographer later took the injured children to a local hospital where it was determined that Kim Phuc would likely die of her burns. But she did not. She spent 14 months in hospital with 17 surgical procedures before she could go home. In 1982 she had further treatment in West Germany.

Kim Phuc eventually defected to Toronto and became a Canadian citizen. She is still known across the world as 'Napalm Girl' and has written several books and committed her life to world peace, a cause that she often journeys around the globe promoting. Phan Thi Kim Phuc has never wavered from her realisation and acceptance that her life from that fateful attack in 1972 was changed forever. She has always been a survivor rather than a victim and used her acceptance to anchor her strength and resilience.[19]

Never ever forget that no matter what happens in your life you still have choices

As we know changes that can impact on our personal and/or business lives are unpredictable and may be frequent throughout our lifetimes. While some of these changes may be anticipated and welcomed, others may be sudden and devastating.

The responsibility and the decision regarding whether you want to be a victim or a survivor is totally up to you and that single decision will from the very outset guide your mindset, your subsequent actions, level of coping, stamina, persistence and ultimately the extent to which you succeed.

Acceptance of change and uncertainty is the first step on the Resilience Ladder. I cannot stress enough the importance of acceptance. It underpins all the other steps.

Denial is the primary obstacle we need to overcome in order to ascend the Resilience Ladder. Without full and genuine acceptance of change and uncertainty, traction and success up the other steps on the Resilience Ladder will always be a struggle, if not totally unachievable.

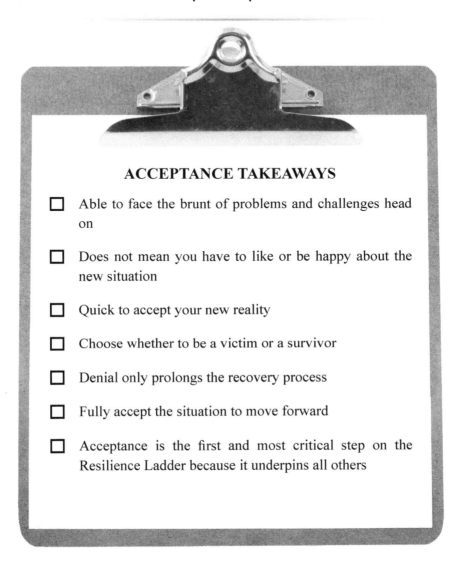

ACCEPTANCE TAKEAWAYS

☐ Able to face the brunt of problems and challenges head on

☐ Does not mean you have to like or be happy about the new situation

☐ Quick to accept your new reality

☐ Choose whether to be a victim or a survivor

☐ Denial only prolongs the recovery process

☐ Fully accept the situation to move forward

☐ Acceptance is the first and most critical step on the Resilience Ladder because it underpins all others

As we absorb the lessons of **Acceptance**, we see that there is a natural segue to our next step that also concentrates on self-reflection: the next step on the Resilience Ladder is **Self-Awareness...**

STEP 2 - SELF-AWARENESS

THE CRANWELL RESILIENCE LADDER ™ - STEP 2

"Fear is self-awareness raised to a higher level.**"**
Don DeLillo[20]

Resilient people possess self-awareness. Step 2 takes us further into some serious contemplation and puts us front and centre on the ladder climb.

When I was in primary school my mother told me, I could become anything in life I wanted to be, if only I wanted it badly enough. I didn't understand what a caveat was then, but I was old enough to appreciate desire alone was no guarantee of success and that a certain amount of talent, skills and diligence might be prerequisites. This became abundantly clear to me as I progressed through school.

At the tender age of eight, I knew I would never make my living as a singer having been removed from the class choir rehearsals for being tone deaf and constantly singing out of key. I had a similar experience in Saturday morning ballet classes when designated to the chorus line… permanently. Oh, the embarrassment and the disappointment. Tennis, netball and athletics went the same way but by comparison my swimming career looked promising.

A tiny taste of confidence

In the water I wasn't hampered by my lack of speed and agility arising from a dislocated hip as a six-year-old. In the water I felt fearless and won several first and second ribbons at our school swimming carnival. Hallelujah! Victory at last.

My confidence soared, only to be smashed in the same year when the families of two of my classmates moved to houses with swimming pools and from that Summer on, they blitzed all my races without mercy. I was flattened again, but I had learnt a most valuable lesson and my short-lived success had given me a new-found confidence and a good dose of reality. I was learning that I wasn't going to be outstanding at everything I tried, but I might find a certain level of satisfaction and enjoyment in other pursuits if I looked hard enough and long enough.

Captain of Enthusiasm

My mother's built-in confidence continued to challenge me throughout a happy but unsensational time at school. I was getting the job done but I always felt that I was more 'Captain of Enthusiasm' than anything else. Finally, in high school I found something I really wanted. I was 15 when I applied (without telling my parents) and subsequently won a Rotary Exchange Scholarship to the US, much to my delight and great surprise. As the Australian and American school years don't match up (we start the school year in January and they start in September) it was a bit like a pre-emptive gap year at another school, the only trouble being that despite the great fun and the mind-blowing experience of spending a year of high school with such confident enthusiastic young friends, I had not even commenced Year 12 back home.

Consequences

There were consequences when I duly returned after my exciting year away, I could not stomach going back to school to undertake Year 12, especially when all my old friends had graduated before I returned home. What followed was learning on the job to become a dental nurse, then studying to qualify as a dental hygienist. I worked happily as a dental hygienist for several years but then I wanted a new challenge. This challenge came with even bigger consequences: I had to temporarily go 'backwards' if I wanted to go forwards. This meant a return to student life, loss of income and living at home with Mum and Dad again to undertake Year 12 to qualify for university entry. It felt a bit like the early success of my swimming 'career' had gone full circle. By then I knew myself well enough to know it was worth the effort to keep searching and find a career that was fulfilling.

Self-Assessment

As a teenager my rather simplistic self-assessment, measurement and resourcefulness had worked, but as a young adult in my early twenties, I realised I had to adopt a slightly more sophisticated approach. When it dawned on me that I didn't want to be a dental hygienist forever and I needed a change in direction I found it necessary to review my fledgling career. I needed to do a stocktake on my life.

The Personal Microscope Test

This crude form of self-awareness developed into what I now call the Personal Microscope Test, i.e., magnifying my skills and attributes against my perceived and actual weaknesses to better assess areas requiring improvement or change. I played this 'game' all the time when I was alone and trying to suss out the future. These days I know it to be a 'visualisation technique' that enabled me to step back and measure myself through my own and others' eyes. I would lie back and picture myself suddenly cast in the role of a laboratory assistant tasked with a forensic examination. Nothing was spared. I was brutally honest with myself. Everything was laid bare on the glass slide as if they were tangible objects. My strengths and weaknesses, achievements, failures, emotional responses, leadership skills, persistence, teamwork abilities and empathy, were all brazenly exposed to see how these skills and abilities aligned with my future dreams and purpose.

Brace yourself - it may be confronting

This can be a confronting experience, but if conducted honestly the ability to self-examine like this on a regular basis can enable us to understand ourselves and others better. It is a very simple method of heightening your self-awareness, but it may provide you with greater insight into what drives you, what you want out of life, where you want to go and why some of us succeed and some of us fall short of our hopes and dreams.

JANINE ALLIS

There is a heading early in Janine Allis' book, *The Accidental Entrepreneur* which reads, "Finding out what I'm made of" and this process is fundamental to her success.

Janine is the co-owner and developer of Boost Juice, one of Australia's most loved juice and smoothie brands. Janine started the business in 2000 with a single store in my hometown Adelaide, South Australia, while on maternity leave. (I remember ordering a 'bespoke' fruit smoothie myself at the store in Rundle Mall when it first opened.)

Boost Juice is now selling in upwards of 600 stores in Asia, Europe, South Africa, South America, India and the UK. Janine is also co-owner of Retail Zoo and she holds an interest in Salsa's Fresh Mex Grill and in CIBO Espresso and is reputedly worth AUD$66 million.

Prior to her business success Janine travelled the world working in numerous jobs, the most notable a two-year stint on David Bowie's yacht. While working in Singapore with very long days, high expenses and tough demanding bosses she learnt how to best judge and support fellow (and future) employees. She learnt the place of integrity in the workplace, the place of high values and where her passions and equally her compassions were best placed. Janine's book is a worthwhile and entertaining read: full of great advice, simple common-sense solutions, witticisms and especially testimony to the significance of self-awareness in the quest for success. Her empathy, her leadership whilst sharing the responsibilities, her unwavering core beliefs and above all her ability to self-examine are paramount.[21]

Business self-examination

There is nothing quite like a crisis or tragedy to highlight a business' strengths and weaknesses. Ideally the level of these capabilities can be discovered and appropriate solutions implemented before, not after, disaster strikes. In business and the corporate sector this examination tool may be referred to as a SWOT Analysis (Strengths, Weaknesses, Opportunities and Threats) or simply a business health check-up, but essentially it is a similar process i.e., conducting a self-examination of the business or organisation's pluses and minuses and the internal and external risk factors that can affect the business.

Internal risks

This evaluation may include but not be limited to scrutinising cashflow, resources and assets, internal risks e.g., ineffective leadership, toxic culture, staff performance, blurred vision and strategies, lack of accountability, employee mental health and wellbeing, teamwork, areas of the business that work in silos and staff that are not empowered.

External risks

External risks factors may include but not be limited to: negative mainstream media and social media, tarnished reputation, confused or negative customer perception, changing/hostile regulatory environment, predatory competitors, environmental and economic factors, closed international and national borders and lockdowns, supply chain failure, difficulty meeting key performance indicators (KPIs) and the business' overall vision and ability to innovate and maximise present and future potential opportunities.

ASHIK AHMED

The *Australian Financial Review* Young Rich List reports that Ashik Ahmed emigrated to Australia from Bangladesh at 17 years old and his first job was to cook burgers in a Melbourne restaurant.[22] *"Ashik was flipping burgers when he arrived from Bangladesh. Now, he's worth AUD $148 million."*[23]

"I was an hourly-paid worker myself so I saw all the challenges on this side, and I also got to see it from the employer's side in managing the employees," Mr Ahmed told SBS News. He combined that experience with his interests in maths and science, which helped him to co-found (with Steve Shelley) a workforce management system called Deputy in 2008. They provide software that aids business-owners to roster and pay their employees. It is a global workforce management platform for employee scheduling, timesheets and communication. Deputy has more than 184,000 single clients and is now used by over 40,000 workplaces in 73 countries, including Qantas and the National Aeronautics and Space Administration (NASA). The systems they have developed help the employees and the shift workers alike.

Now, at 38, Ashik is listed at number 25 on the *Australian Financial Review* Young Rich List, released recently. But for him money was not the driving force and not the outcome. *"I never did it for the money and I still wouldn't. It doesn't matter whether I'm in the rich list or not, it does not change why I get out of bed every morning. Validation in life comes from enriching other people's lives,"* he said. *"I think especially migrant entrepreneurs, my advice to them is that Australia is such a great place to seek out an opportunity and maximise it, and to follow your passion to enrich another person's* life."[24]

The danger of lack of awareness in business

In circumstances where employees feel unappreciated and disempowered, this may lead to resentment and frustration and other negative emotional reactions. If these issues are not addressed appropriately and in a timely fashion, they may fester and spread reducing motivation, decreasing self-esteem, causing loss of job satisfaction and stress, all of which may impact negatively on the culture, productivity and efficiency of the business.

Empathy and leadership

Empathy is a vital component of effective and successful leadership i.e., possessing the ability to identify your own and other people's strengths, weaknesses, emotions and feelings. It is the art of stepping into someone else's shoes and seeing the world through their eyes while not losing sight of your own perspective and objectives to secure the optimum result for the team.

The ripple effect

If there are employees who feel that their voice is being ignored, they are misunderstood, or their work is unappreciated by management it is likely to have a detrimental effect on their attitude and quickly spread like a ripple effect throughout the business. A leader who is finely tuned into their employees' attitudes and emotions has increased capacity to steer them and the business in the direction they need to take it to survive and prosper. This ability to communicate and actively listen applies even more so in disruptive times.

The CEO is like an orchestra conductor

A strong sense of self-awareness will assist the business leader (e.g., the Chief Executive Officer) to identify when to step forward, when to step back and when to delegate with confidence and without fear of revealing a weakness. Let's hypothetically assume for a moment the Chief Executive Officer has changed jobs and is now an Orchestra Conductor. Have you ever seen a Conductor with their back to the orchestra or playing first violin for that matter? No, they may keep an eye on their sheet music, but they are focussed on their musicians and how they are performing. They are not chained to the orchestra pit; they are out front on the raised podium directly facing the musicians where everyone can see them. From this position they can listen critically, unify the performers, set the tempo and ensure that the music is delivered in the way the composer intended.

With a little imagination it's easy to see parallels between these two important roles. Both are striving to achieve an optimum 'performance' from themselves and their people, but in both cases having expertise combined with self-awareness will greatly assist them to lead their people in the right direction to achieve success.

Author, Daniel Goleman comments:

> When Accenture interviewed one hundred CEOs about the skills, they needed to run a company successfully, a set of fourteen abilities emerged, from thinking globally and creating an inspiring shared vision to embracing change and tech savvy. No one person could have them all. But there was one 'meta' ability that emerged: Self-Awareness. Chief executives need this ability to assess their own strengths and weaknesses, and so surround themselves with a team of people whose strengths in those core abilities complement their own.[25]

The importance of delegation

A leader aware of their own strengths and limitations and who is prepared to delegate responsibilities willingly demonstrates that they are not afraid to show that they are human. It also sends a clear message of confidence to the chosen delegates that their leader has confidence in their abilities and that they are seen as the most appropriate person for that aspect of the job. This silences any potential frustration and allows staff to get on with what they do best.

Business silos

A lack of delegation may lead to the formation of business silos that are notorious for causing communication nightmares, costly time delays, inefficiencies, internal conflicts, stakeholder confusion and potentially all-round failure.

Delegating specific tasks to a range of employees with unique skills may avoid the pitfalls of the single 'silo approach' and provide the leader with a better result and broaden their insight into how the business and the people are travelling.

Caleb Bush, Managing Director Senior Vice President, GPJ ANZ and Managing Director ANZ, Project Worldwide said when giving advice about business after winning Managing Director of the Year 2019 and Young Executive of the Year 2019 (*CEO Magazine*):

> **"**... genuinely know what your skills are and bring in people around you who support your weaknesses. Knowing that I am not good at the numbers, I've got an amazing CFO; I'm not good at operations, so I have a great General Manager. I focus on growing the business and promoting and marketing it. Know what you're good at and hire people around you who can support you.**"** [26]

This approach is also shared by Russell Telford, A. G. Coombs' Managing Director for 31 years, when speaking about leadership:

> **"**I think being a good leader is about being engaged. The other important component is Self-Awareness. It's about being conscious that you could be the limiting factor to success if you're not continuing to get the right people around you to continually progress the business.**"** [27]

LEGO

Lego has always been a mainstay for families looking for a children's gift when nothing else comes to mind. "I suppose we can get them another box of Lego bricks," was always the cry. But today it has become so desirable; so specialised into themes, minifigures, gendered characters, engineering marvels, that you need to ask very detailed questions before making a purchase. There are theme parks, television mega competitions – Lego surpassed Ferrari in 2015 as the 'world's most powerful brand'. Pretty amazing to see a toy for children ahead of a toy for very wealthy grownups!

None of this has come by chance. The company and the Kristiansen family who have been with it from the beginning have continually adapted to a changing world and a competitive marketplace. Their self-awareness led them to undertake continuous innovation.

In 1932 amid the Great Depression, Ole Kirk Kristiansen determined that people would still find money for well-made children's toys. In those days they were traditional wooden shapes. The bricks came in 1949, this time defying the market because they were made of plastic.

Big changes were made in 2003 after the first ever losses for the company were posted in 1998. Nevertheless, a review of the competition, such as Mattel, led to new products and operations. Lego dived head first into products the company knew nothing about. The Lego theme parks that they developed cost $125 million and lost $25 million in their first year. The videos games, the dolls, books and clothes likewise. The products connected to the blockbuster films (*Harry Potter*, *Star Wars*) only prospered in the years when the films came out. However, all was not lost.

As recounted by David Robertson,[28] Lego sensationally recovered when newly headed by Vig Knudstorp, who revamped the design, putting the changes in the hands of the loyal international fan base. Lego now conducts the largest study of ethnographies of children in the world for its R&D before introducing new products. They have sold unprofitable activities and responded to the criticism that there were too many new preassembled products that took children away from the experience of assembly. They reinvested in core products, created a Lego Friends line and recognised girls as significant but neglected clients.

Vig (once a kindergarten teacher), who put the 'brick' back into Lego, has always advocated that you must bring your 'heart' to the tough decisions.

For us, this is a prime example of moving from Acceptance, where you admit the need for change to the second step of Self-Awareness, where you examine your strengths and weaknesses, show leadership, listening skills and not a little empathy and reconnect with your core beliefs, values and customer base.[29]

The greatest experience I have ever had in testing my self-awareness came when we received Richard's diagnosis of Alzheimer's disease.

Did I have what it takes and the stamina to lead my family through this crisis? Primitive raw fear hammered at my heart. I was terrified for Richard and our family. I had no idea about how we would cope, knowing that this disease could last for up to 20 years.

Logic Vs. Emotions

Soon I discovered no amount of logic will rescue you from an emotional issue but somehow through the fog that extreme fear creates I managed to identify that what I needed above all else was the courage to accept the diagnosis, the ability to focus on what I could achieve and the strength to delegate and let go of the uncontrollable. In doing so I also had to admit the full extent of my fear, manage it and acknowledge that I could not be all things to all people all of the time.

Practising self-awareness has taught me how to understand and invert my own fears and in doing so it has raised my consciousness and empathy for others around me and especially for those who are struggling too.

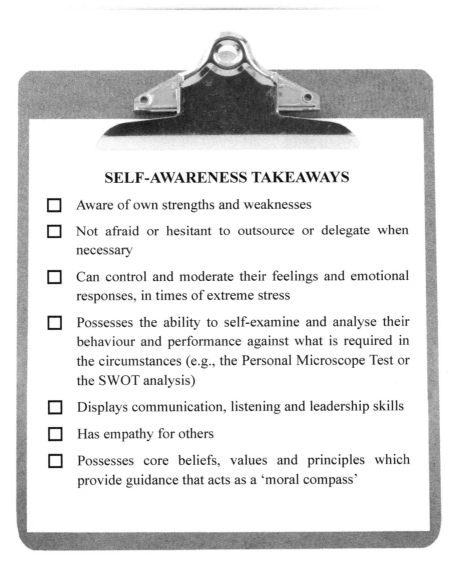

SELF-AWARENESS TAKEAWAYS

- ☐ Aware of own strengths and weaknesses
- ☐ Not afraid or hesitant to outsource or delegate when necessary
- ☐ Can control and moderate their feelings and emotional responses, in times of extreme stress
- ☐ Possesses the ability to self-examine and analyse their behaviour and performance against what is required in the circumstances (e.g., the Personal Microscope Test or the SWOT analysis)
- ☐ Displays communication, listening and leadership skills
- ☐ Has empathy for others
- ☐ Possesses core beliefs, values and principles which provide guidance that acts as a 'moral compass'

Once you have examined your personal or business status quo it is now time to look towards the future in the next step: **Purpose**.

 CLARITY PRECEDES SUCCESS

STEP 3 - PURPOSE

THE CRANWELL RESILIENCE LADDER™ – STEP 3

❝A life lit by purpose is one of clarity and meaning. You don't need purpose when things are going well, but when the tough decisions must be made, purpose points to the answer.**❞**
Nick Craig[30]

❝Live with purpose. Don't let people or things around you get you down.**❞**
Albert Einstein[31]

Resilient people know their **purpose.** This is Step 3 on the Ladder and we are still on the early part of the ascent where we are consciously examining what choices we wish to maintain in our life and in our businesses.

Everyone needs a reason to get out of bed in the morning

Your purpose is central to your meaning and beliefs in life. For many people this is their work or their vocation, for others it is connected to family, their greater role in life and their core values. A purpose is uplifting and often something 'bigger than yourself'.

During COVID-19, countless businesses have had to redefine their purpose and for many that has meant finding a new direction, a new way to survive.

DEBBIE KILROY

Debbie Kilroy has lived a life on both sides of the legal system in Queensland. She had an abusive childhood and married an indigenous rugby player who was excluded from high-level teams because of his ethnicity. The couple sold cannabis before being arrested and while in jail Debbie fought for the right to study. She is now a qualified social worker and practicing lawyer, a recipient of the Medal of the Order Australia (OAM) and the CEO of Sisters Inside who advocate for female prisoners. No stranger to adversity, Debbie is the *"only convicted drug trafficker to be admitted as a lawyer in this country and almost certainly the only person who advocates abolishing prisons to sit on a statutory body guiding governments and courts on criminal sentencing".*[32]

Her sense of purpose is absolute. She is committed, clear and focused on her objectives and will stop at nothing to argue for her strategic visions. In her own words she believes in collaborative leadership, having a *"clear, detailed picture of what [she] ultimately wants to achieve."* Debbie always seeks to understand the social context and advises to *"surround yourself with long term, loyal allies."* All these points feature prominently in the Cranwell Resilience Ladder TM.[33]

Some people discover their purpose in life from a very early age. For example, evidence of their talent surfaces even before they start school or in their formative years. The internet abounds with video clips of talented youngsters singing their hearts out on a television talent show for a chance at fame and fortune, excelling in sport or entrepreneurial feats. But not everyone starts out with a feeling of destiny or knowing exactly what they want to do in life and can't wait to finish school to get started. If they did there would most likely be far less demand for a gap year after high school.

Sometimes we need to look for our lives in lots of different places and try lots of different things. The pathway is not always self-evident the moment you finish your high school education. Mine certainly wasn't. Identifying something that inspires you and that you want to pursue takes time and some inner reflection on your interests, strengths and weaknesses, core values and things you feel passionate about. Generally, the more congruent your choice in career or occupation is with your personality and talents the more satisfied you will feel and the more you will be able to achieve. One of my favourite quotes sums this up beautifully:

"Everyone is a genius... but if you judge a fish by its ability to climb a tree, it will spend its whole life believing that it is stupid. "
attributed to Albert Einstein

Someone who knows their purpose is not easily swayed or distracted from the course they have plotted. Their purpose is often the last thing they think about at night and the first thing they think about in the morning. They see the 'light at the end of the tunnel' but are neither dazzled nor blinded by it as they move towards it. They are conscious of the day-to-day grind but consciously choose not to get tangled up or weighed down by the small stuff. Like a magnet they feel pulled towards their target without overwhelming hesitation or diversion. Of course, purpose-driven people are not omnipotent. They are human and have doubts and fears too but it's their strong sense of purpose that helps keep them in check when obstacles or a crisis occurs.

VIKTOR FRANKL

I first read *Man's Search for Meaning*[34] while at university. Reading it again while writing this book I was reminded how despite the arresting topic, it is so refreshingly honest and easy to absorb. Survival was so natural to Viktor Frankl and his advice to modern men and women is very straightforward: We have a natural quest instilled in us from birth. Life, no matter how miserable and seemingly unbearable can be made bearable by finding your meaning. This was his core belief.

A survivor of four concentration camps during WWII, he was the go-to psychiatrist who offered solace when all seemed lost during the Cold War. Viktor Frankl's books are must-reads. They can significantly enhance your understanding and outlook on life.

To someone with a serious purpose anything less than 100% commitment is not acceptable. If something is not working out quite the way it was intended then adjustments can be made, but quitting is never an option for them. Ask anyone with a true sense of purpose what their purpose is and why they are pursuing it and this will usually elicit a short crystal-clear response. Hesitation and uncertainty don't come into it. However, exactly how they propose to achieve this might initially be slightly opaque, but this will not daunt someone who is purpose driven. A lack of experience is not what they focus on. They'll figure it out by trial and error and adjust if necessary. They know why they want to do something and that is what drives them. Perfectionism may have its place but not at the expense of stalling progress. They recognise that 80% of the work well done is better than costly delays and losing valuable momentum, but the other 20% is far from wasted. Lessons learned will add value to achieving their purpose through increased knowledge and expertise.

American businesswoman and entrepreneur Sara Blakely remembers that her father asked her and her family every week at the dinner table to explain what they had attempted and failed at that week so that they became comfortable with being out of their comfort zone. He encouraged them to try things out, without a guarantee of success and explained that it built their characters, created opportunities and gave valuable skills and life lessons.

SARA BLAKELY

Sara is the founder and owner of a new-age shapewear brand called Spanx. Sara went from having US$5,000 saved by selling fax machines door-to-door in 1998 to being the youngest self-made billionaire in 2012. The increments are just as staggering: US$4M in the first year, US$10M in the second. The rest is modern entrepreneurial 'history' that Sara recounts with the wit and irony of a stand-up comedian (one of her former jobs) and it reads like a 'how to' kit of how to use social media, television and current marketing techniques that circle the globe.[35]

After several failed attempts at getting into Law School, Sara worked as a chipmunk at Disney World, having been rejected from her first choice, the role of Goofy, for being too tall. She then honed her selling skills through selling fax machines door-to-door for seven years. She spent two years trying to come up with an idea for a business, but it wasn't until she chopped off the feet of her pantyhose to keep her silhouette looking trim under her white slacks that she had any idea in which direction her life was going to change.

Solving the problem of *"How to stop the legging rolling up"* inspired her to develop a new fabric that mixes nylon with Lycra. After a lot of hard work and time spent out of her comfort zone, Spanx, the women's undergarment business which has become known the world over, was born.

Sara's 'rags-to-riches' story may sound simple but what followed was a tale of purposeful determination.[36] Sara was very conscious that her mother and grandmother did not have the same opportunities in life that her generation of women did and she was intent on evening the score. She passionately believed women should have a say in developing products, especially products that are intended mainly for women. However, her beliefs did not prevent her from receiving belittling and sexist comments in a hitherto male-dominated industry. As a newcomer to the undergarment business, she found it difficult to be taken seriously. She had to fight to get her patent developed and find a mill to take on her product.

All these challenges just strengthened Sara's resolve and she refused to let them distract her from her purpose or destroy her focus.

Sara credits her father for encouraging his children to 'push the envelope' and for giving her the confidence to follow her 'gut feelings'. She is also generous in praising her network of friends, family and workers for their support. Failing to get into Law School and not landing the Goofy role helped Sara be open-minded about her purpose and she let opportunities and ideas lead her until it all became clear.

The pandemic led to a downturn in sales for the original Spanx products because of the lack of celebratory dress-up events, but rest assured, through Sara's continuous creativity and innovation Spanx has a multitude of various garments on the market. Sara has also stayed true to her purpose and core beliefs through vowing to give away US$5 million to women in need.

Sometimes your original purpose will necessitate a small adjustment or even a quantum leap!

ØRSTED

In 2012, Denmark's biggest energy company, Danish Oil and Natural Gas, slid into financial crisis as the price of natural gas was plunging by 90% and the Standard & Poor's Index downgraded its credit rating to negative. The board hired a former executive at Lego, Henrik Poulsen, as the new CEO. Where some leaders might have gone into crisis-management mode, laying off workers until prices recovered, Poulsen recognised the moment as an opportunity for fundamental change.

"We saw the need to build an entirely new company," says Poulsen. He recognised that the company's original purpose was no longer viable. *"It had to be a radical transformation; we needed to build a new core business and find new areas of sustainable growth. We looked at the shift to combat climate change and we became one of the few companies to wholeheartedly make this profound decision to be one of the first to go from black to green energy."*[37] Poulson named the new firm Ørsted after the legendary Danish scientist Hans Christian Ørsted, who discovered the principles of electromagnetism.

Prior to this the company was a very big oil and natural gas producer. Looking at what their products were primarily used to produce i.e.: energy, they now have become the world's biggest producer of offshore wind energy. The emissions from this activity are zero. They have read the market and the future and repurposed their biggest weakness into their biggest strength.

Of course, the Ørsted story is on the top end of the scale. We can imagine the struggles Henrik Poulson had making such a dramatic transformational change to the company's direction. These struggles are nonetheless also true at the other end of the scale when you are a sole trader or an individual looking for your purpose in life. Finding your purpose is not about taking the easy way out.

MALALA YOUSAFZAI

In 2009, at the age of 11, Malala wrote a blog for the BBC under an assumed name, about what had become her abiding purpose in life: to advocate for Educational Equality for Girls. She was asked to commentate on girls' education in the Swat Valley, a remote part of Pakistan controlled by the Taliban. They had forbidden girls to attend school, especially girls-only schools. Her father operated several schools in the area and he volunteered his young daughter to write the blogs when a number of other girls withdrew.

Malala proved to be an effective communicator and advocate. Eventually a *New York Times* documentary was aired about her life and she gave interviews on television and for newspapers and was nominated by Desmond Tutu for the International Children's Peace Prize. Her true identity was out.

In 2012 while on the bus home from school with her classmates after an exam, she was shot in the head by a Taliban gunman. Malala was initially treated in a Pakistani Military Hospital and after an international outcry she was flown, in an induced coma, to Birmingham UK. After multiple surgical operations she was able to resume her schooling, this time in England. She continued to broadcast her message of peace and equality and gave a speech to the United Nations in 2013. In the same year she co-wrote *I Am Malala,* an international bestseller. That year she also co-founded with Shiza Shahid, the Malala Fund, a non-profit organisation to encourage people to advocate and become activists for girls' education. The following year, then 17 years old, she became the youngest winner of the Nobel Peace Prize.

Malala has now graduated from the University of Oxford, visited Pakistan and continued with her mission to overhaul the problems in international education. She has signed a deal with Apple to produce documentaries and stories to *"reach young women and girls."* This remarkable young woman has been near-fatally shot, threated with further assassination attempts, is loved and hated simultaneously in her home country, yet she has not in the slightest bit deviated from her own purpose. Her strategic vision is clear: danger will not make her quit and her focus is steadfast and true.

It has been said that *"Malala is inspiring because she is speaking up for the rights of those who have no voice".*[38]

A sense of purpose may take a while to develop

Having a strong sense of purpose in life does not necessarily mean that you will immediately know the scale or the final destination in the beginning but don't let that put you off starting. If you are not at least slightly overwhelmed then perhaps your purpose is not strong enough to galvanise your energy, action and long-term attention.

My own journey was not smooth and took some time to work out. If I had not gone to the beach one day, it may have taken me even longer to figure out the direction and purpose that were missing in my life.

Driftwood

In South Australia we are spoilt by stunning coastal scenery and beautiful sandy beaches. Even metropolitan beaches usually have crystal clear water. Typical shells include cockle shells, cuttlefish bones, razorfish shells and various types of seagrasses and seaweed. Sometimes after a storm, the seaweed and seagrasses collect in the shallows and around the water's edge and I have many happy childhood memories of sprinting through nature's spongy obstacle course to get back to the dry sand.

On this particular day I noticed an elegant but gnarly piece of driftwood embedded in a large pile of seaweed. It looked as if it had been marooned after a high tide and was 'patiently' waiting for the current to take it out to sea and continue its journey. It really didn't have any other options of escape. The harsh Australian sun and the salty water made it very weathered-looking and judging by the cracks and furrows I suspect it had been bobbing around on the ocean for some time, perhaps years.

At the whim of ocean currents

I returned to my beach towel and sat there staring, totally intrigued by this rough but beautiful log. How far had it travelled I wondered? How long had it been in the ocean? All sorts of exotic destinations sprang to mind. South America, Africa, India or the Pacific Islands, or maybe it was more local, from South Australia, Victoria, Tasmania or the West?

Aimlessly floating

The longer I stared at it, my interest piqued and the driftwood seemed to have taken on a life of its own. Curiosity pushed my imagination into overdrive. Why had this beautiful piece of timber ended up here when clearly it could have gone anywhere, become anything.? It could have been part of a stylish piece of furniture or a unique sculpture display in an art gallery. It could have been something really special, but instead it ended up here aimlessly floating around the ocean. I amused myself with these possibilities for a while until it was time to go but I was reluctant to leave the beach until I had unravelled this little puzzle and later I realised why. That driftwood was just like me! It was symbolic of my life at that time.

I felt like I too was just floating aimlessly around, knocked about by currents over which I had no control and not knowing my destination or what route I would take to get there. I knew I needed a life-strategy and clarity about my purpose, but nothing was immediately obvious or certain. Time marched on and what followed was a stint as a junior administrative clerk in a law firm, a job as a dental nurse then subsequently study and a career as a dental hygienist.

Not feeling lost, but not feeling found either…

I didn't feel lost, but I just knew deep down I hadn't found the answer and sense of direction I was looking for. Some years passed and from time-to-time memories of the day at the beach and the driftwood returned but I still hadn't discovered the answer. By chance I attended a party where a group of young friends were discussing what changes we would make in our lives if we suddenly won a fortune in the lottery. Joking, I said I would buy a luxury yacht and sail around the world.

When the internal alarm bells start ringing

To my surprise, some of my friends said they would keep doing exactly what they were already doing at that time, like going to university or working because they were enjoying it so much. This triggered my internal alarm bells because although I was not unhappy in my job, I couldn't imagine spending the rest of my life cleaning teeth and staring at tonsils.

I found myself at the crossroads…stuck somewhere between a dead-end street and a detour. There didn't seem to be any way around it…. It was time to go under my personal microscope again.

Going back to move forwards

This led me to fulltime study to complete Year 12 high school (to make up for the year I spent overseas) and then into Law School at the University of Adelaide. This was no quick fix. It meant four years full-time study or eight years part-time. It was a big commitment, but I felt mentally and emotionally prepared for it.

Finding a purpose worth fighting for

My introduction to Law School however, came as a bit of shock when in the Welcoming Address we were advised to turn and have a look at the people in the lecture theatre sitting around us. *"On average only one in four will successfully complete the law degree..."* The Dean of Law continued, but he didn't need to say anymore because I had spent the last year preparing for this day and I was already in fight mode. *"Well, that won't be me,"* I thought as I glanced at my neighbours, *"because I'm not budging."* I had finally found a place where I wanted to be. I knew my resolve was going to be seriously tested, but I believed I had found a purpose that was worth fighting for. I finally had a clear direction in my life and something that I could focus on.

I no longer felt I was aimlessly floating around the ocean or shooting at a moving target. It was a huge relief. My 'Driftwood Days' were officially over.

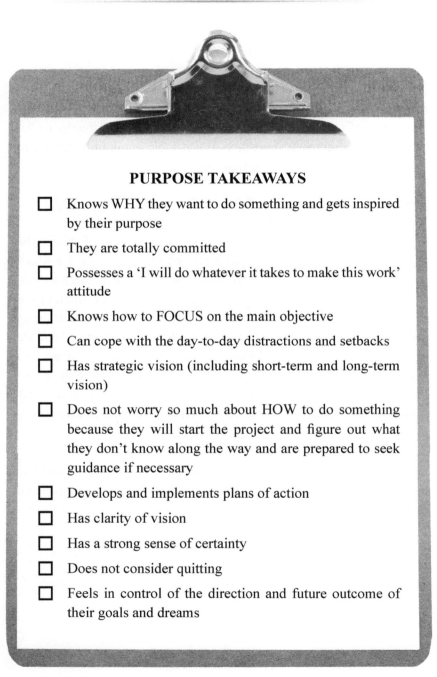

PURPOSE TAKEAWAYS

☐ Knows WHY they want to do something and gets inspired by their purpose

☐ They are totally committed

☐ Possesses a 'I will do whatever it takes to make this work' attitude

☐ Knows how to FOCUS on the main objective

☐ Can cope with the day-to-day distractions and setbacks

☐ Has strategic vision (including short-term and long-term vision)

☐ Does not worry so much about HOW to do something because they will start the project and figure out what they don't know along the way and are prepared to seek guidance if necessary

☐ Develops and implements plans of action

☐ Has clarity of vision

☐ Has a strong sense of certainty

☐ Does not consider quitting

☐ Feels in control of the direction and future outcome of their goals and dreams

We are about to ascend to the middle step of the Resilience Ladder now, where we learn one of the secrets of success in business and life: **Flexibility**

STEP 4 - FLEXIBILITY

THE CRANWELL RESILIENCE LADDER™ – STEP 4

> **"**The measure of intelligence is the ability to change.**"**
> **Albert Einstein**[39]

> **"**Invert, always invert. Turn a situation or problem upside down. Look at it backward. What happens if all our plans go wrong? Where don't we want to go, and how do you get there? Instead of looking for success, make a list of how to fail instead. Tell me where I'm going to die, that is, so I don't go there.**"**
> **Charlie T Munger (Business partner of Warren Buffett)**[40]

Resilient people are **flexible** in their outlook and in their practice.

Flexibility is the next step on the Resilience Ladder. This step requires us to understand that sometimes circumstances dictate that we must make changes to stay on track in our businesses and in our lives.

Across the world we hear stories of companies whICH have had to adapt to stay relevant in the marketplace to survive. The people in those businesses have learned to 'flex' in response to internal and external events.

The best made plans often don't turn out the way we intended. As Simon Sinek says, we should *"always plan for the fact that no plan ever goes according to plan."* History teaches us that those who are prepared to welcome change and be flexible increase their chances of survival and success in business and their wellbeing in life. Those who are unprepared to be flexible or are in denial of the need, risk failure or being left behind.

It is in this context that we look at Flexibility as the next step on the Resilience Ladder.

IGNITE DIGI

Ignite Digi was started in 2013 by Chris Fox and Tom Waugh, from an aeronautical and cinematography background. With 97% of their products being exported overseas to support the film industry they initially found the Covid 19 a crisis too far. But showing the agility and inventiveness of a flexible company they quickly circumnavigated the obstacle by turning from lenses to shields. Personal protective equipment (PPE) was in very short supply and so they switched to producing protective face shields for essential medical services. This diversity should see them through until the export market comes on track again. This business model has been seen the world over and hopefully teaches us new lessons that being flexible is a key skill for now and into the future.[41]

The digital business era has arrived whether we are ready or not

The so called 'good old days' of certainty, when people often worked in the same job or business for their entire lives have all but disappeared. Mass production, electronics, information technology and the evolving digital revolution have all contributed. Our world has been changing so rapidly that today the ability to change, be flexible and innovative are essential skills in business and in life. Artificial intelligence, 3D printers, automation software, drones and self-driving vehicles are just a few examples of technological innovations that are about to transform the way we interact with the world and each other. This is not a time for a rigid approach. We need to be able to bend and sway like a palm tree in the breeze or during a violent storm.

An agile approach

Constant change requires constant innovation. If you are not agile or flexible keeping up with your competitors won't be an issue for long. They will sail right past you.

A strategic, agile, flexible approach that embraces change and marries business innovation with technology is essential but simply updating technology and modifying operations alone is not the sole answer. Agility must be embedded throughout the business strategy and culture.

How agile and innovative are your leadership team and your employees (because they will be the ones implementing these changes)? Can they bend and not break?

Sometimes flexibility is forced upon us

The Stagekings story below is a classic example of flexibility on steroids!

STAGEKINGS

Covid-19 was literally the show stopper for Stagekings' Jeremy Fleming. In Melbourne, Victoria, with a 23-staffed company, the curtain came down on gatherings of over 500 people.

And it just happened to be Friday the 13th.[42] The Formula One Grand Prix 2020 stage rig for the Robbie Williams and Miley Cyrus concert was cancelled. Over on another site, the Ninja Warrior set for Channel 9 was in limbo, as was the set up for the Twenty20 cricket. After two days of cancellations Jeremy and his wife and business partner, Tabitha had to come up with a new plan urgently.

Next is a tale of ultra-flexibility. Jeremy, using his hobby interest in furniture teamed up with the company Head of Production, Mick Jessop and designed a flatpack desk to fill the need of those suddenly forced by the pandemic to work from home. Tabitha with her marketing acumen set up an e-site and 30 desks sold in 24 hours.

The rest is a survival success story. Their flexibility saved them from financial disaster. Within days Stagekings had morphed into IsoKing. There are now 70 on the staff. Like the business of a true entrepreneur, IsoKing was quick to 'pivot'. They recognised almost immediately drastic change was essential.

Their response was agile, innovative and creative. They capitalised on their strengths and resources available to them and they worked their way through uncertainty without caving in.

The IsoKing desks and other products…. (yes, the new business is rapidly growing) can be assembled and deconstructed in 30 seconds, no screws, no staples. The desks are agile in themselves and still echo the quick bump in and bump out of the concert staging process. Perfect for the new instant solutions that the pandemic has forced upon us.[43] From world-class custom staging on a grand scale to customised indoor furniture on a tiny scale. That's impressive flexibility!

However, being flexible is much easier to talk about than do.

It requires silencing the 'Oh, but we've always done it this way' and the 'It's worked for us before' comments and introducing people into a whole new way of thinking. For many, it's so tempting to stick with the familiar and well-trodden path, especially if change is only 'in the wind' and has not yet arrived at your front doorstep.

3M

The 3M corporation started life as a mining company but despite initial failure, went on to become a Fortune 500 company consisting of four distinct business groups: safety and industrial, transportation and electronics, health care and consumer products.

Historically the secret to 3M's survival lies in its ability to continually flex, adapt and transform itself. Strong leadership and a culture that was open to new opportunities, coupled with an environment that encouraged staff creativity enabled them to design innovative new products. Under the guidance of William McKnight, it was acknowledged that not all initiatives or products would be successful. However, it was accepted that mistakes made in product development might not cost the company in the long run as much as the mistake of management killing off or stifling staff creativity.[44]

3M's philosophy may seem counterintuitive to other corporate operators but by fostering a company culture that embraced continuous flexibility, the 3M company has been able to produce products such as scotch tape and post-it notes that have become international household names.

With approximately 60,000 products in 2019 and over 100,000 patents 3M, the corporate inventor, has more than 100,000 patents worldwide[45]. 3M has repeatedly proven its strength and phenomenal success is derived from rejecting a rigid 'set-and-forget' mentality in favour of a 'flex and bend' philosophy and culture.

Learning flexibility often begins in your personal life

Being a flexible thinker doesn't require a degree in rocket science or membership of Mensa. It can start with the smallest of steps. If you are flexible at home, chances are you will be flexible in every aspect of your life, including your attitude at work.

Being time-poor taught me to be flexible, to 'mix it up' and adopt a less rigid lifestyle. As a young wife and mother of two I frequently found myself time poor, but I was still intent on obtaining a university degree. There just weren't enough hours in the day to accomplish everything I needed to do. I knew I still only had the same 24 hours as everyone else, but I had to find a way to s-t-r-e-t-c-h my day.

Reframing

I did this by thinking about time differently. I needed to crib a few extra hours. I decided a more flexible approach and a 26–28 hour day would suit me perfectly. The first thing I did was ditch the traditional 9 am – 5 pm routine and opt for the 24-hour clock. I divided my 24 hours into six-hour units that suited me better. Six hours for sleep left the remaining 18 hours to be arranged any way I wanted: six for family time and the remaining 12 hours would be split across study and household chores. I didn't have the luxury of a live-in housekeeper like my grandmother, but I did have a lot of appliances my mother and grandmother never had when they were raising their families.

Rallying the household 'staff'

Reflecting on their lives, I realised I had a whole team of household 'staff' right at my fingertips. I had an automatic oven, a dishwasher, a microwave oven, an automatic washing machine and a clothes dryer, all of which I discovered performed equally as well before midnight as they did after. I set my new 'staff' extremely flexible rosters. They could work early morning or late-night shifts and simultaneously if required. They could even work when I wasn't in the house to supervise them. It was a very convenient arrangement.

Reframing my perspective on time and 'staff' was liberating. As a family we learnt that meals cooked or laundry done at midnight do not taste or look any different to that prepared during more conventional hours and when the pressure of exams and end of term deadlines loomed late-night ironing became a great way to think and plan assignments while the rest of the 'staff' worked quietly and the house was still and peaceful and the telephone didn't ring.

After that experience flexibility became second nature. It was a mind-shift not a mindset that enabled me to successfully pursue my dream.

Flexibility comes with practise

The flexibility skills I had developed during my Law School years became invaluable later in life when Richard's Alzheimer's progressed. As his symptoms escalated from mild to moderate to severe, we seemed to lurch from one crisis to the next, ranging from frustrating domestic events to a life-threatening heart attack, violent seizures and frequent falls in the later stages. Living in crisis mode became our new normal. It was essential that we became seriously flexible and inventive on the home front as a matter of survival. When our daily coping mechanisms worked out, we celebrated them and when they did not, we focussed on finding new ways to approach the situation. This constant extremely unpredictable behaviour prevented attachment to any particular strategies or coping techniques, so being flexible and innovative became second nature to all of us.

MATT AND AMANDA CLARKSON

Many people dream of changing their entire lives but Australians, Matt and Amanda Clarkson, actually did it. They realised early that online retail marketplaces like eBay would give them the opportunity to quit their jobs and work for themselves from the comfort of home. They epitomise the agility, creativity and resourcefulness of flexibility on the Cranwell Resilience Ladder ™. Matt worked as a carpenter on a range of building sites, Amanda in dozens of jobs but always with an eye out for entrepreneurial success. Life brought them to a place where they had to make a change and they accepted the challenge. Now they run eBay education programs based around their business called Bidding Buzz. It continues to operate no matter what the circumstances… another strength of flexibility![46]

A crisis rarely happens when you are ready for it

Have you ever noticed that no matter how prepared you might think you are, a crisis rarely happens when you are ready for it? Odds are it's very unlikely to happen when the sky is blue, the sun is out, the birds are singing and when everyone you need to talk to is either seated at their desk or ready and available to take your call. If they were, it would likely be an incident rather than a full-blown crisis.

After nearly 20 years' experience in government, I have found that a crisis usually happens when the weather is foul, nearly all the relevant executives and 'gatekeepers', including the subject matter experts and your industry contacts are either away sick, on annual leave or you can't reach them immediately on their mobile phone.

When your fail-safe system fails...

So, when your fail-safe system fails; that's when you need to be innovative, resourceful and extremely flexible. You need to view your situation from all angles, quickly assess the risks and consequences, the extent and duration of the impact and recovery, canvass a selection of possible actions, then pick one and run with it!

Counter-Terrorism security and emergency management experience

For over 15 years I provided advice on counter-terrorism security measures, physical and protective security, security risk management, security plans, security awareness, culture, training and personnel security clearances to the State Government transport department. This included providing advice on how to minimise security risks at government transport buildings, depots and facilities e.g., physical entry and access controls to buildings, lighting, intrusion detection systems, CCTVs, and at critical infrastructure sites, physical barriers, gates, fencing, site hardening (appropriate stand-off distance between the critical asset and the nearest point of attack) and other crime prevention measures. All these measures are necessary and help deter security breaches and build organisational capacity and resilience but alone they are not enough. Employees at these important sites need to know how to react and act when faced with a security incident or a potential crisis.

Exercises help to develop strength and flexibility

Part of my work required preparing relevant employees for the possibility of such events. This necessitated planning, writing and facilitating hypothetical counterterrorism and emergency management exercises for mass passenger transport systems e.g., for trains, trams, buses and ferries. These exercises tested the operator's security plans, incident and crisis response, management, internal and external communications, resources and asset management, engagement with government, networks, industry stakeholders and first responders such as police, ambulance, fire and emergency services and business continuity arrangements.

Field and discussion and exercises

There are two principal formats by which these exercises are delivered, namely field and discussion exercises. Field exercises are conducted on a large scale and budget and they require staff and volunteer participants to act out the hypothetical scenario and respond to the requirements of their role as they would in a live terrorist incident. This can take from six to twelve months preparation.

Round table discussion exercises are more common and are conducted regularly. Typically exercise participants would not be briefed on the scenario until they arrived at the exercise venue where they would be gathered in a large meeting room and presented with a hypothetical situation. Groups would then discuss their security plans, roles, responsibilities, preparedness, response and recovery arrangements against the challenges presented in the scenario.

Hypothetically speaking...

My fictitious scenario might read something like this:

"Federal Police have advised all jurisdictional Rail Commissioners across the country that they have received credible information from government intelligence agencies about a plan to conduct a terrorist incident at a major metropolitan train station late on a Friday afternoon

*of the upcoming long weekend. Some states are currently experiencing a blistering heat wave. The Bureau of Meteorology has advised there is no end to the extreme weather in sight. Catastrophic fire warnings have been issued in three states across the country. Emergency services will be stretched to maximum capacity in these jurisdictions. Police cannot rule out a secondary incident may take place on a train scheduled to arrive or depart during peak hour. The identification of the State, the station, the rail operator and the route are currently unknown. All State and Territory Government transport departments and private transport operators are advised to be on high alert, review their security plans and activate their highest security measures. In the event of a security incident be prepared to take appropriate actions. **Do not wait until Police or Emergency Services arrive as their resources may be stretched to maximum capacity.**"*

In the heat of the moment…

Participants would then discuss a series of simple questions which might commence with 'How do you react?', 'Who do you tell?', 'What are your first steps?' These might seem like such basic questions and that their answers should be automatic but in the pressure of the moment it is not always as easy as it may seem in hindsight. Department officials and transport operators are faced with the daunting task of making major decisions potentially affecting their staff and shutting down public transport which may be the only means of transport for thousands of people for an unspecified time. Many standard procedures would apply and their application and implementation would often be vigorously discussed, but there was no point to the exercise if it did not challenge the participants' flexibility, creativity, innovativeness and resourcefulness.

The importance of keeping the pressure up

To get the most benefit from the exercise and simulate what is required in a real-life situation, we needed their adrenaline fired up but so they were still able to function properly. If the discussion got bogged down on technicalities and started to stall, a nod from me to the exercise facilitator would signal time to inject a twist or two into the scenario that would really get their hearts pumping. Fortunately, most participants took these exercises seriously and this type of 'forced motivation' was not required, but if it was the added twist might look something like this: *An international sporting match is scheduled for the following day in your city. City hotels are overflowing with visitors, teams, coaches and media. The match will be broadcast live internationally."* Bigger crowds than normal and heavy media and social media attention is always guaranteed to turn the pressure valve up a notch or two!

Always expect the unexpected and then you will never be surprised...

In writing the exercise some facts in the script would be deliberately kept vague to build in the element of surprise and uncertainty. This would require participants to think broadly, address multiple considerations and to develop more than one solution in case the first one didn't work. The good news is that participants are advised before they start that no one ever fails an exercise because they are designed specifically to practise routine procedures, flexibility and innovation, to educate and to build strength and capacity.

To understand your adversary, step out of your shoes and into theirs...

One difficulty I encountered in conducting these exercises was occasionally getting some participants to mentally inject themselves 100% into the scenario and to anticipate the terrorists' modus operandi. This is understandable, because acts of terrorism are so foreign to our way of thinking and behaviour. A terrorist intent on achieving mass casualties does not worry about speed limits, traffic lights, road rules or smashing their way through low level landscaping and garden beds, closed gates, fences or even deliberately ploughing into crowds of people, e.g., Bastille Day truck attack in Nice, France 2016. Their focus is on inflicting as much death and destruction as is humanly possible. They prefer surprise. The attack is designed to shock, create fear, exploit vulnerabilities, cause mass casualties, create economic loss and generate as much international publicity for their cause as possible.

There are so many potential variables....

Given the often surprise nature of a security incident even well thought out security plans may not always fit the situation, even with a variety of built-in contingencies. This is not exclusive to security breaches and incidents. The shock factor may apply whether you are dealing with a terrorist incident, a business crisis or a serious personal situation. Whatever the event, flexibility is a key skill and essential when you are confronted with a significant issue and many unknowns. The ability to do a complete mental U-turn and implement that decision is by no means an easy feat for most of us and requires practice not only in business but in our personal lives too. Taking on new work challenges and hobbies that require you to think outside the square, continuously improvise and problem solve is a great way to hone your flexibility skills.

Flexibility skills can be learned

Being flexible in our thoughts and in our actions is a conscious choice but it may not come naturally or easily to all, especially when circumstances arise that challenge established practices, traditions or attitudes. However, the skill of being flexible can be learned and practised and the best way to do that is by regular exercise, i.e., putting yourself into situations where you need to be able to quickly reassess a situation from many different angles, think on our feet and carry out innovative adjustments as needed.

In this global era of uncertainty, a failure to be flexible may derail any chance of achieving successful sustainable resilience. History shows us that poor flexibility can be a decisive factor in determining which businesses and which people rise or fall.

FLEXIBILITY TAKEAWAYS

☐ Agile and original thinker

☐ Quick to respond to crisis or change

☐ Resourceful

☐ Can come up with multiple solutions, i.e., not one dimensional

☐ Creative

☐ Innovative

☐ Adaptive

☐ Can circumnavigate serious obstacles

☐ Can continue to operate and function at a high level even in times of great uncertainty and potential or very high risk

☐ Can continue to flex as the circumstances demand and for as long as necessary

☐ Will not cave-in or snap under pressure

Next, we climb to Step 5 to learn how to sustain our progress with a **Positive Mindset...**

STEP 5 - POSITIVE MINDSET

THE CRANWELL RESILIENCE LADDER™ – STEP 5

> **"**Change your thoughts and you change the world.**"**
> **Norman Vincent Peale**[47]

> **"**I am a very positive thinker, and I think that is what helps me the most in difficult moments**"**
> **Roger Federer**[48]

Resilient people always keep a **Positive Mindset**. This Step has less of the intense self-questioning of the previous one. This time we need to dig in, find some trust and keep our eyes on the goal.

The Doubt Squad

Towards the end of university my motivation started to fade. I was beginning to doubt myself like never before. Despite many sleepless nights, I managed to keep my head just above the waterline with my studies and tutorials. It was a challenging time for me. Although I had successfully completed substantially over 75% of the degree the 'Doubt Squad' in my head was growing louder every day.

After a year of pre-university study, immediately followED by six consecutive years of part-time Law School you would think I would have been able to read the signs that I was exhausted. I did not.

The Cheer Squad

Throughout this entire period my mother and husband had been my greatest supporters and even though they never said it, I could see it in their eyes, the 'Cheer Squad' was getting a little tired too. Although I was the one doing the study, their contribution in enabling me to do so was not without sacrifice. Richard carried the major financial burden of supporting the family and paying for childcare. My mother helped when her health was good with home-cooked meals when I had an exam or assignment due. I cherished their love, support and sacrifice.

The Cheer Squad Vs. The Doubt Squad

Looking after my husband, our daughter, a new baby, studying and juggling a few shifts as a dental hygienist, I have to admit I was pushing it. However, one of the downsides of being self-driven is there was no one to blame but me! All of this was voluntary. No one was holding a gun at my head and forcing me. By 'burning the candle at both ends' I was losing stamina and emotional steam and didn't know how to refuel. The tussle playing out in my head between the Doubt Squad and the Cheer Squad was wearying to say the least.

Friends and extended family would say encouraging things like, *"You must feel great now that the end is nearly in sight."* I would smile back at the well-wishers as I thanked them for their support, but all the time the voice in my head which was growing fainter and weaker every day whispered back *"...Yes, IF I can just make it to the finish line?"* I was spending way too much time 'inside my head' and the isolation was palpable.

Running on empty

During these final years I spent many hours in the library which was decorated in drab grey décor, complete with uncomfortable chairs, musty air, cold fluorescence lighting and situated in the basement of the Law School. One of its saving graces in my opinion was that it was located across the road from the CBD so if I got desperate to escape at lunchtime it was reassuring to know some retail therapy was available in case of 'emergency'. On one such day, I decided to go for a walk to clear my thoughts. I didn't really have any specific destination in mind but somehow, I wandered into one of the few remaining book stores in Rundle Mall. There I was approached by a very friendly and chatty shop assistant. Time to 'fess up' I thought. I admitted I was an escapee from the university who was running on empty and needed something motivational to pick me up. I must have looked incredibly flat because I was immediately escorted upstairs to the Self-Help section! Wow! I didn't realise I came across as that much of a train wreck.

Quickly I graduated from the Self-Help to the Business Development section and then I oscillated between the two. What a revelation!

Aladdin's Cave

I flicked through book after book. So many stories of successful people who had overcome all sorts of tragedy and major obstacles in their businesses and personal lives. Better still, they were prepared to share their wins AND their losses with anyone who cared to read their book. Amazing! I felt like I had found Aladdin's Cave and it was full of sparkling treasure. I flicked through book after book, engrossed by what I discovered. Success (and a healthy dose of failure) had left a massive trail of evidence everywhere I looked. There was so much to choose from. I flashed my credit card. It was a feast!

Suddenly I felt like a total wimp. There were endless stories of people who had coped and triumphed over far greater obstacles than I was facing. Their enthusiasm and energy were contagious. Interestingly while some had experienced failures, they never really saw themselves as defeated.

I hadn't even failed. There was hope for me yet!

Reading Moratorium

A few months earlier I had been wondering if I needed to see a doctor or psychologist to help lift my spirits. But Aladdin's Cave was full to the brim with motivation, inspiration, coaching and strategic advice and all for approximately $19.95 per book. I decided then and there to place a full 12-month moratorium on any reading material (excluding my law books) that did not inspire, motivate or train my mind to think in a positive way. This self-imposed embargo extended to magazines, novels and even recipe books. Evening television viewing time was also restricted. I picked out one favourite program a week to enjoy with my husband and apart from the evening news that was on while I prepared the evening meal, that was it.

My new best friends

The positive impact was just about instantaneous. I started to look on people like Tony Robbins, Napoleon Hill, Jack Canfield, David J. Schwartz, Stephen R. Covey, Harvey Mackay and Norman Vincent Peale like my new best friends. I couldn't wait to get home at the end of the day and on weekends to 'hang out' with them.

I was astonished but delighted that they had made themselves so readily accessible and couldn't believe the difference their company and knowledge brought to my life. It felt amazing. Burdens became 'challenges', failures became 'learning tools'. The Doubt Squad completely vanished along with the isolation. My stamina returned and I couldn't stop smiling.

Never underestimate the power of a Post-it Note...

I still didn't have any more hours in the day than I had before, but I learnt to prioritise my time better.

I wanted to ensure that I could spend time with my mentors every day. Might sound corny, but I wrote the words 'YOU can do it' on a yellow Post-it Note and put it on the bathroom mirror so that every day began and ended on an encouraging note and strengthened my self-belief.

The negativity that had occupied and threatened to take over precious 'real estate' in my mind had been booted out. A new powerful positive army had moved in and I was back occupying the 'driver's seat'. Hallelujah!

Back in control

It was such relief to feel back in control of my destiny and I vowed never to succumb to such negative feelings again. No matter what happened in my future now I knew how to deal with doubt and negativity and I refused to let them win.

After the 12 month moratorium was completed, I eased up on my targeted reading. The positivity saturation strategy had been successful, more than I had ever actually anticipated. I was transformed. The bathroom Post-it Note remained in place but instead of questioning it, I believed it and it gave me the strength I needed to get safely to the finish line.

TURIA PITT

After graduating as a mining engineer in 2010, Turia Pitt was competing in an ultramarathon through the Kimberley region in northern Western Australia (a rugged mountain, gorge and arid semi-savanna area) in September 2011. Her working and athletic life lay before her. She was happy and confident.

Unfortunately, the race organisers had very poor communications in place and a fast-running grass fire suddenly swept up a gorge and crossed the course, giving the competitors no alternative but to run through the inferno. Turia suffered burns to 65% of her body. She was airlifted out two hours later with no expectation of survival.

In an induced coma for one month, Turia lost most of her fingers, stayed in hospital for six months and had 200 medical procedures in the next two years. I recently heard her say on television that there are still more operations to come. She is at one with her new appearance and remains confident.

Turia is an Ambassador for ReSurge International (formerly Interplast) and has helped raise $1 million for the organisation by leading trekking adventures, including walking the Great Wall of China (2014), the Inca Trail (2015) and the Kokoda Track (2016). The organisation volunteers free reconstructive surgery to Third World children. She is now a motivational public speaker in high demand, has written three books and has been interviewed countless times. She has competed in an Australian Ironman Competition and in the World Championship in Hawaii.

Australia has embraced Turia for her bravery and amazing recovery and for her witty insights which are meaningful and uplifting but always down-to-earth. She credits her mother, family, partner Michael and the birth of her two sons with helping her to recover, not to mention the medical staff all over Australia.[49]

But what makes Turia so positive and so *'abundantly happy'*, as she puts it?

She says that her *'voice'* to survival was *"always there in her head...you just look forward and wake up tomorrow... you take your wins where you can...and the responsibility is always on YOU despite all the help* (from others, especially her Mother). *As a child, if struggling with something like maths and you were so frustrated and you said, 'Mum I can't do it', and she'd say, 'no Turia, you can't do it yet'".*[50]

Turia plays to win, yet is truly grateful. She has a remarkable sense of humour and while realistic, maintains an expectation to succeed. That is what I call a Positive Mindset!

Marathons

In any long-term endeavour enthusiastic supporters frequently love to point out how easy it must be now that the finish line is almost in sight, but chances are if you ask any marathon runner which part of the race is the toughest, they will tell you it's the last few kilometres when their mind and body are spent and their spirit is beginning to flag. This is perhaps the most dangerous and vulnerable time when despite committed ambition, physical fatigue is undeniable and self-doubt threatens to jeopardise finishing the race.

The marathon I was competing in wasn't in a sports stadium, it was at university, but there was no world class coach by my side or roar of the crowd to cheer me on. There was no prospect of podium glory or gold medal either. All my effort was for an A4 size piece of paper with my name stamped on it and a ticket to an uncertain future.

Casting Call: Major role for inspirational heroine

One night I was up 'burning the midnight oil' and wrestling with a law essay that was due the next morning. In the kitchen waiting for the kettle to boil it occurred to me that what I needed was an inspirational heroine that I could 'call' upon when my energy tanked. "Yes, that would work!"

I was convinced of it. Now who to choose? I needed someone strong and successful. Someone who could be depended on in a crisis, someone with an unwavering spirit and enduring sense of commitment.

Pick one and run with it…

Tea was made and I was back at my makeshift desk on the dining room table when the name of one of drama's most famous characters popped into my head. Don't ask me why but Lady Macbeth turned up. Now she was hardly the exemplary role model I was looking for but certainly someone strong and determined which is all I really needed at that moment. Why I didn't think of Joan of Arc or Mother Teresa I'll never know but time was marching on, my deadline looming and sleep was beckoning so the audition for strong female lead went to Lady Macbeth that night. I could always arrange another casting call back later if things didn't work out!

Having sorted that little conundrum out, work progressed and I finished the essay just in time to get a few hours' sleep in before the alarm went off and the family's usual morning routine commenced. Phew! Down to the wire, but I got there. Thanks Lady Macbeth. Perhaps all those nasty things people have been saying about you for centuries are exaggerated? No time to research this, I just had to keep moving.

Shakespeare, The Monkees and David Cassidy

Now to add to my 'special' talent for choosing female role models, my memory and understanding of Shakespeare's sonnets and verses was equally unreliable. Whether or not the hours my 13-year-old self, spent looking out the window during English Literature class dreaming of pop group The Monkees and pop idol David Cassidy contributed to my literacy capacity at the time is hard to say, but with the benefit of hindsight I suspect it contributed to the 'accuracy' of my memory of some of Lady Macbeth's qualities and famous lines.

Enough to make Shakespeare turn in his grave…However, I never felt inclined to revisit Shakespeare after that year in junior high school. Why would I in fact when 'Daydream Believer' was storming the music charts and David Cassidy was such a superstar?

I distinctly recall thinking Shakespeare was not a good match for me, although many years later I was particularly grateful for the few lines I could recall: *"But screw your courage to the sticking place, and we'll not fail."* This worked really well because it made courage seem like a tangible object and all I had to do was bolt my courage down and it would not desert me. So far so good.

My mantra

Now my memory of the second line was not quite so sharp, nonetheless it turned out to be equally effective and for the last half of my law degree when my spirits started to flail, I would repeat it over and over again. *"In firm of purpose"* became my mantra. I translated this to mean strong and staying focussed which was exactly the panacea I was looking for.

A most valuable lesson

It wasn't until many years later that I finally looked up the quotation and to my horror discovered the line was actually *"Infirm of purpose"*, i.e., there was no space between *in* and *firm* and the correct meaning was not firm purpose as I had believed, but weak willed and lacking in spine, the complete opposite to my empowering mantra! I laughed till I cried at my own foolishness and ignorance (while simultaneously begging Shakespeare's forgiveness), but all was not lost because I learnt a most valuable lesson: the power of having a Positive Mindset and believing. You see it didn't really matter that my heroine was an evil woman and I had chosen in extremely bad taste. It also didn't matter that I had Shakespeare's meaning completely wrong. The fact that I believed they were empowering words gave me strength when I needed it and that is all that mattered. It doesn't hurt to have a laugh at yourself either and I still laugh every time I think about this today.

Empowering beliefs

Rest assured, I am positive you will do a much better job than I did at choosing a heroine or hero and remembering Shakespeare accurately, but even if you don't – just believe you have. It's sounds crazy, but it actually works!

GILL HICKS

"Time hasn't masked the memory, nor the fact that I will never physically recover, my legs will never grow back."

At 8.50am Gill Hicks was running unusually late. She was always in the office at 7.30 am. She was sleepy after a disturbed night and was hardly concentrating when the explosion ripped apart her carriage. The young 19-year-old terrorist took his own life, the lives of 26 others, grossly injured 340 and Gill lost her legs from the knees down. Across London the carnage continued in four simultaneous attacks. Gill recalls a beautiful calming voice of 'death' encouraged her to give up and *"come"*, while a commanding male voice urged her to stay and fight on.

She was labelled **"Unknown One"** and the resus team were seconds away from giving up when she flickered back to life.

In Gill's own words: "*It was a Thursday morning and there was some light rain, typical of a London summer's day. I remember running to catch the train, frantically weaving through the swarm of morning commuters in Kings Cross Station. There must have been three rows of people standing on the platform, all eagerly awaiting the next train. I was so pleased with myself that I managed to push through to get to the front of the queue. When I close my eyes I can still feel that rush of wind on my face that signifies an underground train is coming down the tunnel. As I stepped onto that carriage, I wasn't to know that boarding with me was a 19-year-old man who intended to detonate a bomb that was concealed in his bag. I didn't see him. I didn't take in the detail of anyone in our carriage. I guess I was conditioned by the unwritten rule of commuter etiquette in London – no eye contact and absolutely no talking! The doors shut.*"

In that blackened, shredded carriage while the survivors waited in agony for an hour Gill resolved to respond in some way if she survived. She knew somewhere in this life-changing event lay a seed…

"*The bomber didn't know me, this attack wasn't personal – no – in order for him to carry out his mission he placed us all into a convenient group – we were 'the other', the 'them' as opposed to his 'us' and by doing this he was able to see us not as individuals or fellow human beings, but as his enemy. I knew instinctively that the vow I made in the carriage to make a difference was exactly what I needed to do, so I left my career within architecture and design and created a not-for-profit business, called Making a Difference for Peace (M.A.D).*

My focus was to do all I could to deter anyone from falling under the influence of destructive extremist ideas… building a sustainable peace is, I believe, our collective responsibility. I would like to raise my child in a world whose people were empathetic and actively engaged in peace as part of their everyday."

While not understating the time and struggle taken to recover it has been said that Gill was amazingly quick to rehabilitate. She quickly graduated from a wheelchair to the prosthetic legs that she uses today.

This speaks to the heart of having a Positive Mindset. Gill had (even at the scene of the explosion) a high level of optimism, she was courageous and very balanced and logical in her resolution of what to do about terrorism.

"My life was saved that day and, in many ways, every day since, by the selfless and courageous actions of the paramedics, the police, the many people who were prepared to place the life of a stranger, someone unknown, above their own, in order to save and preserve life. What I received from them is the power of human interdependency, interconnection and the unbiased love that ultimately binds us all."

Gill did not return to her old life in London, where she had once been publisher of *Marie Claire*, then a design consultant and finally the Head of Curation at the UK Design Council. She has instead returned to my own city, Adelaide where she is married with a little girl, works as an inspirational speaker and runs her non-profit organisation for world peace, M.A.D.

Gill's memoir is *One Unknown* (Pan Macmillan, 2007).

Gratitude helps build ongoing resilience

Despite having experienced all manner of trauma and challenges those with a strong positive mindset like Gill are able to recognise and distinguish good situations from bad and turn their focus towards the positives. Gill's positive attitude demonstrates that gratitude expressed either privately or publicly can provide an enormous sense of healing and wellbeing. The power of practising gratitude emotionally and mentally fortifies us for tough times: gratitude helps our brains build a protective barrier against negativity and loss of hope.

"Gratitude is like a good tenant in the real-estate of your heart and mind. The more gratitude you have the more property it occupies, leaving less room for accommodating the bad tenants – the negative thoughts and emotions that can bring you down.**"**
Carolyn Cranwell

STARBUCKS

Seattle, Washington, USA is known the world over for its spectacular scenery and flourishing entrepreneurial culture and spirit. Visitors are always shown around to where the famous World's Fair was held, the mindboggling enormous Boeing development fields, Microsoft and the famous fish auctioneers stall at the Pike Place Market. Nearby is another famous 'first'. That is where Starbucks started trading.

Founded in 1974, by three coffee-loving friends, Jerry Baldwin, Gordon Bowker and Zev Siegl, Starbucks was named after the first mate on Captain Ahab's ship in *Moby Dick*. It was principally a coffee bean and equipment supplier, inspired by Alfred Peet, who traded in San Francisco. It was riding the wave of new ideas in the 1970s that saw the West Coast spearhead the new age in America of institutional challenge, experimentation, travel and acceptance of new ideas, that included new foods and beverages. The outlets slowly grew in Seattle until Howard Schultz came on board in the 1980s and, after a trip to Milan came back bursting with ideas of espresso bars with coffee and light foods. For the next two decades you could find a Starbucks on many street corners in many world cities that served coffee and tea and not just packages of fragrant beans.

Starbucks exists today as a potent force in street life and café culture around the world. The first decades of the company show a partnership, growing into a corporation that had very strong core beliefs. They helped increase wages for workers, searched for sustainable products and stayed true to their aims of supplying good coffee and tea and building world's best practice roasteries in several cities. Their positive mindset is the envy of many companies. They were trailblazers who tapped into an emerging trend and still play to win in a now crowded market.[51]

POSITIVE MINDSET TAKEAWAYS

☐ Possesses high level of optimism accompanied by realistic perspective (i.e., filtering system)

☐ Confident

☐ Courageous

☐ Balanced approach to life and work

☐ True to their authentic self

☐ Success orientated i.e., starts out expecting to succeed

☐ Continually practices gratitude

☐ Takes pride in success but maintains humility i.e., has healthy attitude towards success and does not get distracted or carried away by their own success

☐ Sense of humour even under highly stressful circumstances

☐ Not afraid of competition

☐ Not threatened by team environment i.e., comfortable with their own abilities and recognises some situations require multi-skills approach

☐ Not threatened or intimidated by others' success

☐ Has a healthy and balanced risk appetite for challenges

☐ Plays to win

We have completed Step 5 and now we come to everyone's Achilles heel: **Persistence**

STEP 6 - PERSISTENCE

THE CRANWELL RESILIENCE LADDER™ – STEP 6

❝Nothing in this world can take the place of persistence. Talent will not; nothing is more common than unsuccessful men with talent. Genius will not; unrewarded genius is almost a proverb. Education will not; the world is full of educated derelicts. Persistence and determination alone are omnipotent.**❞**
Calvin Coolidge[52]

Resilient people exercise and master persistence to get what they want. We are all guilty of 'dropping the ball' from time to time but when we find our natural capacity for persistence, we are all amazed at the results… but it takes patience and practice.

Read almost any book about someone who has become successful in a specific endeavour or their chosen field of interest and you won't have to dig too deeply to discover that they have been persistent in pursuit of their goals or dreams. Persistence requires a dedicated form of self-discipline and control.

Someone with persistence knows their purpose and is blind to the myriad distractions that could daily throw them off course completely. They use their vision to keep themselves on track. They have three types of vision: short-term, long-term and peripheral vision.

Success depends on how you view failure

Persistent people often have a unique attitude towards failure in that they perceive it to be merely a guidance tool and an opportunity to correct and reset. The risk of failure does not rattle or discourage them, in fact they expect some failure as part of their learning curve.

Pacing yourself is important

To be persistent you need to push and pace yourself so that you don't burn out, because anything truly worthwhile may take an investment of time and energy. You don't have to charge ahead blindly, just continually monitor your progress and adjust your plans when and where necessary.

There may be an element of luck, BUT…

How often have you heard conversations about someone becoming incredibly successful and you hear comments like 'Oh, they got lucky' or 'They got into business at the right time or 'They were in the right place at the right time'? Similar phrases to this effect are so common in fact that I think it is frequently believed that they are legitimate reasons that explain, justify and distinguish why some people succeed against the odds and why some people don't. True, there may be an element of luck involved and good timing may play a part as well, but usually if you look behind any success story, you'll find someone who has done a lot of hard work and persisted through tough times, disappointments, rejections, setbacks and even failure.

Persistence personified

Many famous people have become household names today, not just because of their talent and achievement, but because they have refused to give up and have spent time to reach their goals and dreams. In other words, they are also famous for their persistence:

Thomas Edison said, *"I have not failed 10,000 times – I've successfully found 10,000 ways that will not work."*

Now a literary superstar, **J.K. Rowling** had her manuscript rejected 12 times before a publisher agreed to print the first book in the *Harry Potter* series.

English war-time Prime Minister, **Winston Churchill** recognised that there was no shame in failure when he said, *"Success consists of going from failure to failure without loss of enthusiasm."*

An engineer and medical physician, **Dr Mae Jemison** is the first African American female astronaut. She has worked as a specialist scientist aboard the Space Shuttle Endeavour. Despite the discouragement from several teachers and the lack of peers from her own background she went on to gain tremendous qualifications. Before joining NASA, she worked in Africa in the Peace Corp and with refugees in Thailand.

Colonel Sanders, the founder of Kentucky Fried Chicken fast-food chain faced 1,009 rejections before finding success at the age of 62.

Sir James Dyson, inventor of the world's first bagless vacuum, had 5,126 failures but he refused to give up before he achieved success.

Marie Curie overcame childhood poverty and educational prejudice against women in Poland to be the first woman to obtain a doctorate in science at the Sorbonne in Paris, the first woman to win a Nobel Prize and then the first person to win two Nobel Prizes. She discovered radium and polonium (which ultimately shortened her life) and made huge steps towards the therapy for cancer.

Chinese internet business giant, **Jack Ma**, the founder of Alibaba Group, failed his college entrance exam twice and got rejected from Harvard University a record ten times.

As Zig Ziglar says,

"When obstacles arise, you change your direction to reach your goal; you do not change your decision to get there.**"**

JACK CANFIELD

Jack Canfield is an American author, entrepreneur, businessman, multimillionaire and co-creator of the international best-selling *Chicken Soup for the Soul* non-fiction book series.

The story of how Jack achieved a stratospheric level of success in business and in his life is nothing short of inspirational. Jack has spent his life helping others transform and massively improve their lives through teaching his 'Success Principles' based on his own life-experience.

It is tempting to focus on Jack's current success and think he has it easy, but it wasn't always that way. Like so many others before him Jack learnt the hard way. Persistence played a critical role in achieving the resilience he needed to reach a level of success beyond his wildest dreams.

Jack mastered the art of persistence through mastering:

- his mindset
- his skillset, and
- choosing to be surrounded by positive, knowledgeable and inspiring people (e.g., Clement Stone)

When Jack and his co-author, Mark Victor Hansen, sought a publisher for their book, *Chicken Soup for the Soul*, they had no way of knowing they would have to search for about a year and endure over 130 rejections. Publishers just weren't interested in a collection of short stories with what they perceived to be lacking in 'edge', but Jack and Mark understood the secret to success lies in not giving up. They refused to let other people's lack of vision destroy their vision and commitment to their dream.

After failing with New York publishers, they attended the American Booksellers Association convention in Anaheim, California and "walked from booth to booth, talking to any publisher who would listen."[53]

They understood that getting published was an endurance race and that every time someone said *"No"* to them, they just said *"Next!"* After two very long days and much worn-out shoe leather, they finally found a publisher who agreed to take a risk on their book. Jack recalls, *"Those hundreds of 'nexts' had paid off. After over 130 rejections, that first book went on to sell eight million copies, spawning a series of eighty best-selling books that have been translated into thirty-nine languages."* That one *"Yes"* transformed their lives and created a brand worth over $100 million dollars, including products such as pet food, a soup, and greeting cards.[54]

Rejection does not mean that you have failed

The purpose of this story is to help you realise that when someone rejects your manuscript, or you don't get the job of your dreams, or the bank rejects your loan, or you can't find investors to get your start-up company up and running, you still have a choice. You can see it as a temporary setback or a final one depending on how you handle the rejection. Jack's story teaches us that rejection does not mean that you have failed.

Rejection won't kill your dream

Rejection doesn't have to be terminal. Your dream will have life for as long as you believe in it. Yes, guaranteed rejection will test the depth of your belief, but as author, Ken Blanchard wisely points out, *"There is a difference between interest and commitment. When you're interested in doing something, you do it only when it's convenient. When you're committed to do something, you accept no excuses, only results."*[55]

Rejection is hard. None of us are thrilled by it, some of us even live in fear of it and hate it, but it's our attitude and the techniques we use to handle rejection that enable us to keep going when our inner voice is shouting time to quit and end the humiliation.

How do we sustain our motivation and rise above the nightmare of repeated rejection?

Firstly, we start by acknowledging that while it may be entirely possible, it is unlikely that we are going to hit the jackpot on our first attempt. Numerous attempts may be required. Then it is critical to reframe any potential rejection into something 'palatable' to your risk appetite and ability to withstand failure.

Rejection can be a two-edged sword

Instead of focussing on what you have missed out on, focus on the magnificent opportunity that someone has missed out on by not hiring you or accepting your proposal. Do you think some of the publishers who knocked back Jack and Mark might have had some regrets down the track when *Chicken Soup for the Soul* became a sensational success story and then morphed into a series of very successful books and products worth millions? And really do you want to be working and building business relationships with someone who couldn't see you or your project's true worth and potential?

In the words of Jack Canfield, *"When the world says no, you say, next."*

Success is not negotiable

Never in the history of medal winning Olympians did an athlete have a conversation with their Coach that went like this: *"Well, sorry Coach, I can't come to training on Friday night because there's a football game on TV that I want to watch and on Saturday night I have a hot date and on Sunday morning I might be hungover."* Elite athletes understand that success is not negotiable. They know that the price of success is not a question of what they are prepared to put in. The price of success is whatever it takes to achieve their dream. Outstanding success rarely happens overnight (in any endeavour). It takes dedication, concentrated effort, patience and persistence beyond the ordinary, but it **IS** achievable.

SIR JAMES DYSON

"I made 5,127 prototypes of my vacuum before I got it right. There were 5,126 failures. But I learned from each one. That's how I came up with a solution. So I don't mind failure. I've always thought that schoolchildren should be marked by the number of failures they've had. The child who tries strange things and experiences lots of failures to get there is probably more creative."[56]

The Dyson Vacuum Cleaner has become famous because it doesn't lose suction when it fills up with dust. It uses cyclonic separation and does not use a bag. James Dyson was frustrated with his Hoover and put his considerable design skills into a new concept. He borrowed a feature he had seen at a sawmill. His new idea worked (5,127 models later) but new concepts can find it tremendously hard to get traction. In 1983 he had to try the Japanese market. His hot-pink model was given an industry design award. It took another three years to gain a US patent. It was still impossible to get the manufacturers to take it on, so in 1993 the Dyson Company was born to produce his revolutionary product. The company is worth many billions today and Dyson continues to invent and nurture new and innovative design the world over.

Where did this persistence come from? It was obviously a very difficult time in his life and that of his family. They lived on his wife's art teacher salary and it took 15 years. Sir James puts it down to determination and as I quoted earlier, his respect for trying things that can fail. He recounts his experience with long-distance running, at which he was very good, *"I was quite good at it, not because I was physically good, but because I had more determination. I learnt determination from it."* It is recounted that during this challenging phase of his life, he also lost his father in a protracted battle with prostate cancer.[57]

Persistence requires you to stay true to your core beliefs, true to your dreams and ambitions and get back on your feet every time you get knocked back and knocked down. In Sir James Dyson's case he would get back up, make a few adjustments and try again.

We are all familiar with the term to "Hoover" meaning vacuuming the house and referring to the dominance of the Hoover company's product. It may not be long before that catchphrase is replaced by "Dyson"!

Marshmallows and Self Control

Those with the greatest self-control may find persistence easier to achieve. In the 1960s renowned psychologist Walter Mischel, conducted an experiment with young preschool children at Stanford University's Bing Nursery School to detect the presence or absence of self-control. The children were given the choice between one treat (e.g., a marshmallow) or if they waited and resisted the temptation to eat the enticing marshmallow right in front of them, they could gain a bonus one and eat two marshmallows when the teacher returned. But to win this reward they had to wait alone in the room for an indeterminate time (which could be up to 30 minutes) without eating the treat. At any time, they could ring a bell and the teacher would come back and they could eat the single marshmallow.

However, ringing the bell immediately meant that they had to forfeit the bonus marshmallow. Their behaviour and results were observed and recorded well into adulthood, and it was later found that *"the more seconds they waited at age four or five, the higher their college-admission SAT scores and the better rated social and cognitive functioning in adolescence."*[58] Interestingly, this pattern of success continued throughout their lives.

J.K. ROWLING – 'RAGS TO WITCHES'

The J.K. Rowling success story was made by a fairy-tale called *Harry Potter*. She developed the synopsis of the seven-part story while seated on a delayed Manchester-London train. As a single mother in difficult circumstances, it must have come as a blessing to concentrate on something so exciting, so all-encompassing with just a little smidgeon of hope in the future for publication. When you spend so much time with books and language as she did, she must have known in her heart of hearts that she was on to something.

What follows is one of the most written about modern day stories of persistence. The first book and the synopsis of the complete series was rejected 12 times until it was referred to Bloomsbury Publishers who took it on. Prior to this Rowling worked in research after university and worked as a bilingual secretary. She had a job in Portugal, married and had a baby, however the marriage was abusive and divorce followed after a year. Upon returning to Scotland, J.K. often sat in coffee shops to keep warm and rock her baby to sleep whilst penning the first book. She was suffering clinical depression and in her own words, *"By every usual standard, I was the biggest failure I knew"*.[59]

The *Harry Potter* series of books have continually topped the bestselling book chart in many languages (500 million) and the film franchise has been a huge success. It is said that *Harry Potter* is worth $US15 billion and J. K. Rowling would still be on the Forbes Billionaire's list in the UK, but she keeps giving money away.[60]

Rejections often bring out our persistent best and it is said that aspiring authors become experts at exercising the kind of patience and self-belief that accompanies persistence.

Delayed gratification can be learned

While some children may have found the marshmallow experiment easier than others, it does not mean that the principle of delayed gratification can't be learnt if the person is willing enough. This principle plays a major role in mastering persistence. Exercising self-control and enduring delays and sacrifices are frequently required in the pursuit of a dream. Persistent people accept this as part of the process and do not see these elements as barriers. Test yourself out by putting a block of chocolate in the fridge on Monday and see if it survives the week. If you really truly want to fit into that wedding dress or special occasion dinner suit, chances are the chocolate will still be there on Friday.

It's not magic

Often persistent people are accused of 'being born like that' but there really is no magic trick to developing persistence. You doggedly pursue a dream. Sometimes despite your best efforts you face setbacks; however, you are not discouraged by rejection or failure. If you 'fall off your horse', you get straight back up again. You find another means to get you where you want to go.

Persistent people often reap huge dividends. Sara Blakely never became a lawyer, but she did become an incredibly successful businesswoman and a philanthropist.

The good news

I've saved the really good news till last…

It's FREE!

Anyone can be persistent if they choose to and you can start today.

You don't need to come from a privileged background, be born with a silver spoon in your mouth, look like a supermodel, play sport like an Olympian, be a social media superstar or have a PhD.

It's on the table right now…

It's a choice, it's a decision, it's a commitment and it's all there ready for the taking.

Once you know exactly what you want then there is only one question you need ask yourself:

Q. How badly do I want this dream?

Are you willing to pay the price, if the price is *whatever it takes*? Big dreams are rarely 'cheap' or for that matter easy so be prepared for some hard slog.

Head and heart

However, if you answer "Yes" then you are on your way. If you hesitate, start to hedge and negotiate terms and conditions, then maybe it's time to keep looking. In my experience it is almost impossible to persist with anything for a long time if your head is in it, but your heart is not. If your heart is involved that changes the landscape considerably.

Key drivers

Passion and purpose drive persistence. Perfectionism sometimes kills it. People who are persistent learn to live with their mistakes and imperfections. They are also forgiving and kind to themselves and usually to others. They don't waste unnecessary time with recriminations or beating themselves up for getting off track or errors of judgement. Setbacks and mistakes are never fatal in their eyes. They are far more interested and focussed on pursuing their dream. But persistence doesn't just come down to diligence and hard work. Plenty of people can do that. It's a blatant test of desire. Those who have something to prove or want something badly enough that they will keep going against the odds, against the competition and against all their fears. It's the hungry ones who succeed the most.

The giant step

There is a good reason why persistence is the penultimate step on the Resilience Ladder. I believe that persistence is a crucial factor in measuring personal resilience and success, because it is like a giant step that incorporates all the preceding steps i.e., Acceptance, Self-Awareness, Purpose, Flexibility and Positive Mindset. If you can master these steps, persistence will flow and you will be well on your way to achieving sustainable hardcore resilience for life.

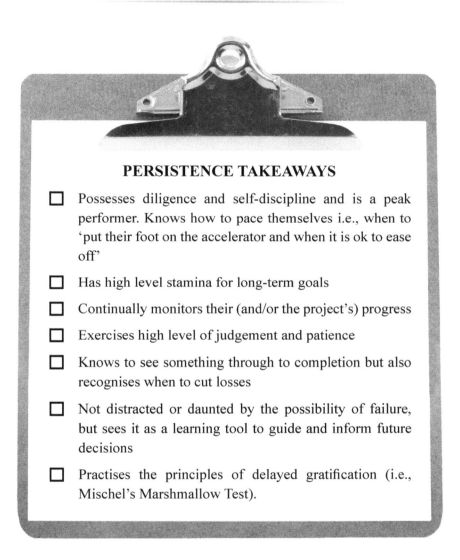

PERSISTENCE TAKEAWAYS

☐ Possesses diligence and self-discipline and is a peak performer. Knows how to pace themselves i.e., when to 'put their foot on the accelerator and when it is ok to ease off'

☐ Has high level stamina for long-term goals

☐ Continually monitors their (and/or the project's) progress

☐ Exercises high level of judgement and patience

☐ Knows to see something through to completion but also recognises when to cut losses

☐ Not distracted or daunted by the possibility of failure, but sees it as a learning tool to guide and inform future decisions

☐ Practises the principles of delayed gratification (i.e., Mischel's Marshmallow Test).

We have almost reached the top of the Resilience Ladder; next we discuss what it takes to stay there.

STEP 7 - STAYING CONNECTED

THE CRANWELL RESILIENCE LADDER™ – STEP 7

"No Man is an Island,

Entire of itself.

Every man is a piece of the continent

A part of the main

If a clod be washed away by the sea

Europe is the less

As well as if a promontory were

As well as any manner of thy friends or of thine own were

Any man's death diminishes me

Because I am involved in mankind

And therefore never send to know for whom the bell tolls

It tolls for thee."

John Donne[61]

Resilient people work hard at **staying connected.** In this final step we seek to consider our connectivity, our wellbeing and to maintain the lessons we have learned on the Resilience Ladder.

John Donne wrote *"No man is an island."* This could not be more true in the quest for human survival. Our cave dwelling ancestors found safety and wellbeing in numbers and generally this preference for human proximity and interaction remains universally true today.

Strictly speaking Staying Connected is more of an overarching concept than a literal chronological step, however I believe its inclusion on the Resilience Ladder is essential. It is imperative that we recognise and remember the extent to which our lives are intertwined and how our relationships with others impact on nearly every facet of our lives. Staying Connected pervades every step on the Resilience Ladder and serves as a constant reminder to us of the importance of our relationships as a support and wellbeing system not just when we are struggling but throughout our lives.

When climbing the Resilience Ladder it is vital to reach out to others and stay connected. Your connections may include family members, friends, co-workers, neighbours, university lecturers, school teachers, fellow students, your industry professionals, co-workers, acquaintances and members of your sporting, religious, hobby or community groups or anyone else who can support you in the process.

The impact of isolation

Imagine your life with your business struggling or closed and your family, friends and community suddenly distant or gone. When everything is going well it is easy to take our connections for granted as if they will always be there, but should your circumstances suddenly change you will very quickly know who and what matters most if the threat of losing them is real enough.

TANYA HOSCH

Tanya Hosch is a Torres Strait Islander woman who lives in Adelaide. She is the General Manager of Inclusion and Social Policy at the Australian Football League and has distinguished herself for many years in Aboriginal and Torres Strait Islander policy, advocacy, governance and fundraising. Tanya was a crucial contributor to the National Congress of Australia's First Peoples, and a foundation director of the Australian Indigenous Leadership Centre and the Australian Indigenous Governance Institute and until recently also served on the Boards of Bangarra Dance Theatre and the Australian Red Cross. Recognised separately as a 'woman of influence' by Westpac, the *Financial Review*, the *Women's Weekly* and Price Waterhouse Coopers. She is the 2021 South Australian of the Year.

When a prominent national TV host and Australian Football League club president upset the public over racism announcements, we learn that it was prompted by a report conducted by Tanya and she was the first person that the media went to for comment. She is helping to build new social infrastructures for our whole nation.

We can see from her endeavours (and I have only brushed the surface of her public work and awards) that Tanya dedicates herself wholly to staying connected to her people and to connecting other Australians with First Nation peoples.

"I've been fortunate in my career to have opportunities and platforms, and if I've got those, I should be using them for things that really matter".[62]

Connectivity strengthens our resilience and our well being

Staying connected with people who we know care about us and who we care about can help with many business and personal challenges such as stress, fear and loneliness, uncertainty and sense of purpose, anxiety and depression, self-image and self-belief, motivation and boredom and many more.

One of the most repeated catch cries of the pandemic has been "We are all in this together." Knowing there are people to turn to when our business or life is struggling can be a great comfort and confidence booster. They may be able to offer helpful advice or just provide a sounding board for you to let off steam and decompress. Either way having reliable trustworthy support is easier than going it alone and it may substantially increase your mental health and resilience.

A digital connection is better than no connection

People who lived through the Spanish Flu did not have the advantage of digital connection like we do today. While nothing replaces face-to-face contact, video calling, video conferencing, video concerts, social media, online groups and classes have kept our lines of communication open and our world a closer place. I live in Adelaide, South Australia and my four year old granddaughter and infant grandson live 16,254 kms away in London. Due to Covid-19 travel restrictions I could not be there this past December but we video call every week and I was able to watch my granddaughter opening her presents in 'real time' on Christmas morning. Absolutely priceless! It is not the same as being there, but I am so grateful for the technology that afforded me the opportunity to see her excitement on Christmas Day.

Dig your well before you are thirsty

From the start of your connection genuine acts of thoughtfulness and appreciation will go a long way towards building rewarding personal, customer and client loyalty. A positive pre-existing relationship is a lot easier to maintain during a lockdown or crisis if it has been nurtured since Day One. Work on developing strong networks across the most pertinent areas of your business and personal life and creating genuine lasting stable relationships.

People like to be asked

For some, reaching out is the hardest part but it will be even harder if you wait until a crisis occurs. Generally, people like to be asked to help and find it flattering that their knowledge and insights are considered valuable by others.

Communication is key

Regular communication can be the lifeblood of your business even when there is little or no progress to report. That may sound counterintuitive but sometimes people just want to be reassured you are there for them. They prefer to be forewarned about any delays or lack of supply but most importantly they want to know that you haven't forgotten them or misplaced their order. A goodwill phone call can keep the customer or client relationship alive until product supply or services can be resumed.

When working as a Ministerial Adviser to the Minister for Planning, Infrastructure and Local Government an anxious developer contacted me regarding progress of his application which was before the State Government planning authority. The proposal involved a large project and complicated infrastructure and the developer was under increasing financial pressure. In my role as a Ministerial Adviser, I could not do anything to speed up or influence the approval process in any way but what I did do was telephone the developer every two weeks just to let him know I was tracking his application and it was in progress. I was unable to give any further information whatsoever. The developer understood this, but he was just so relieved and pleased when he received my calls. He could talk to a real person and he knew he hadn't been forgotten and his application wasn't 'lost in the system'. Finally, after many months when the project was approved, he thanked me profusely and said it was my phone calls that helped him survive this stressful time. *"I would have cracked if it hadn't been for you. I couldn't have got through it without your help,"* he said. It made a huge difference to his mental health and wellbeing yet all it had cost me was a three-minute conversation once a fortnight and with no actual news or valuable information to report.

Keep your key connections close

Early in my career as a government Security Adviser, I participated in a national counter-terrorism mass passenger transport exercise. The scenario was hypothetical, but our instructions were to operate as if we were in a real-life situation. As the day progressed, my need for urgent information intensified.

I became frustrated by not being able to get confirmation from relevant officials regarding updates on the number of fatalities and horrific injuries that were flooding into my office. I needed accurate, authenticated information to write up an urgent status report. Once the exercise had begun to heat up my local contacts were impossible to reach by mobile phone or landline and they weren't responding to emails. My backup contacts could not be reached either.

The exercise scenario was time sensitive so I needed to speak to someone urgently. I started calling my interstate colleagues who were also participating to see if they had any senior connections with major national transport operators that I could access. In a real-life incident, calling interstate to verify what is going on in your own backyard seems a drastic way to operate but that is the situation I was confronted with on that day. It is often assumed that in a crisis people's availability will operate just like normal, but that is not always the case. Depending on the scope and volatility of the circumstances and the incident location they may be overwhelmed, out of range or mobile phone services are just unable to cope with the number of calls.

Eventually I got the information I needed by a rather circuitous route, but it was time-consuming and like pulling teeth and it left me concerned about what could potentially happen in a real-life incident. Prior to the exercise I would have said my connections were strong and up-to-date but this exercise clearly demonstrated they were not as reliable as they needed to be in a catastrophic disaster. To prevent this situation arising again (even if only in another hypothetical situation) I organised a group of key emergency officials to ensure that we stayed connected regularly and could all gain the fastest and most direct pathway into our relevant departments and agencies at a moment's notice.

HOWARD TUCKER CBE

Now a retired police detective, Howard Tucker tells a remarkable story that characterises many of the steps on the Resilience Ladder that we have previously read about and demonstrates the importance of staying connected to your support network.

Howard was raised in a loving supportive family and he was one of six children. He was particularly close to his older brother Gareth who was paralysed at 11 years of age when his spinal cord was severed (during an operation to remove a life-threatening growth). In my conversation with Howard, he recalled with great pride and fondness how Gareth never let his disability define who he was and that he was *"the single most influential person in my life."*

Howard gained a strong reputation in the South Wales and later the Gwent police in Wales in the 1980s, where he was often called to do the difficult autopsy viewings, not being fazed by the grimness of the task. During these years he kept in touch with international police news and secondments, but little did he know that just a short tourist flight away, Bosnia was rapidly plunging into a violent civil collapse to rival the savagery of mediaeval times, or the Nazi death camps in the 1940s.

The history of this region is complex. The death of Tito, known to many as the benevolent Communist dictator who stood up to Stalin in 1980, left Yugoslavia without the glue that held the once-warring states and ethnic groups together. But it was not until 12 years later, when Soviet Communism disintegrated, that civil conflict broke out across the region. After independence was declared for Bosnia Herzegovina the remade Yugoslav Army with a heavy Serb presence attacked the Moslem community, especially targeting men and boys. Initially in 1993 they casually slaughtered 120 in Central Bosnia, by 1995 that had risen to 14,000 including the Srebrenica Massacre of more than 8,000 civilian men and boys. The situation became very complex with eventual Croat militias forming and it is naive to characterise it as simply Serb atrocities. More recent estimates are 100,000 deaths for the whole war, with 2.2 million people displaced.

Howard Tucker applied for secondment and was finally appointed in 1998 as an investigator for the United Nations International Criminal Tribunal for the former Yugoslavia (UN ICTY) into allegations of Genocide, War Crimes and Crimes against Humanity.

Howard was subsequently appointed as a full-time investigator to the UN ICTY, obtaining a five-year career break from the Gwent police before he ultimately had to resign from his police career at the end of his career break in 2004 to take up various UN posts that lasted until he was required to retire from the UN at the mandatory age of 62 in 2013. By then he was Head of Mission for UN ICTY in Bosnia and Herzegovina. His work included taking witness statements, verifying them, exhumations in Northern Macedonia, supervising autopsies, securing local areas from threatened attack and work in Kosovo. He recounts how he, as a male policeman from the UK, had to gain the trust of often distrusting Moslem women via translators. He often had to return to very reluctant witnesses time after time to convince them of the importance of gaining evidence for a conviction. Sometimes he had to go well beyond his brief, thinking on his feet when emergencies and violence occurred to aid the mission. Another difficulty was preparing the teams for the grizzly task of the exhumations. Firstly, the forensics of the search, because to hide atrocities mass graves were often dug up and the victims moved by the perpetrators and reburied and then the detailed examination of murdered victims.[63]

The eventual results were more than 160 soldiers and leaders from the military and paramilitary units, police officers and politicians were brought to trial in the Hague, amongst them some very infamous names: Ratko Mladic, Radovan Karadzic and their deputies, and Zdravko Tolimir. A slow, painful and painstaking task but a very important one. Howard actively participated in about 20 of those arrests and subsequent trials. He well deserved his Commander of the Order of the British Empire award (CBE), bestowed on him by Prince Charles and awarded "for services to international justice".

Howard calls his survival, resilience with a good mix of stubbornness. During his time with the UN, he had cause to panic on numerous occasions because of the unfamiliarity of the situations that presented, but he just had to *"shake himself mentally"* to concentrate and manage the crisis. Back home he was soundly supported by his wife and loving family, whom he could only see briefly every six weeks. Before his last posting he had to compromise his police retirement pension by his early resignation. His wife however insisted, saying that she would go back to work herself to make ends meet as this was so important to him. Fortunately, a UN pension eventually filled the gap. Throughout his challenging career Howard has always stayed connected to the people that mattered to him most and his strong network of friends and work colleagues whose support helped him fulfil this most important role.[64] Howard is currently writing his story and we look forward to reading a lot more from this brave, resilient Welshman.

Your connections, whether personal or business are the glue that links, holds and binds everything we value in life together. Human beings are by nature social creatures and psychological wellbeing is related to your social support and connections with family and friends, work colleagues and associates.[65]

Nowadays there are many ways to stay connected: telephone, video chats and meetings, text messaging, email, social media, write a letter, but never underestimate the impact a gesture such as a phone call or catching up for a coffee, may have on the recipient. It may help someone to avoid giving in to tragedy or disaster.

> **"**At home we lived in our Alzheimer's bubble but our connections with the outside world, although tenuous at times, is what saved us all from being victims.**"**
> **Carolyn Cranwell, *Navigating Alzheimer's – Survival Secrets of a Long Term Carer.***

Connections can be with people, places, occupations or endeavours – anyone or anything that mentors or supports you or speaks to your sense of wellbeing and self-worth. Turn towards and not away from the connections in your life. Staying connected to the people in your life might one day just end up saving your life.

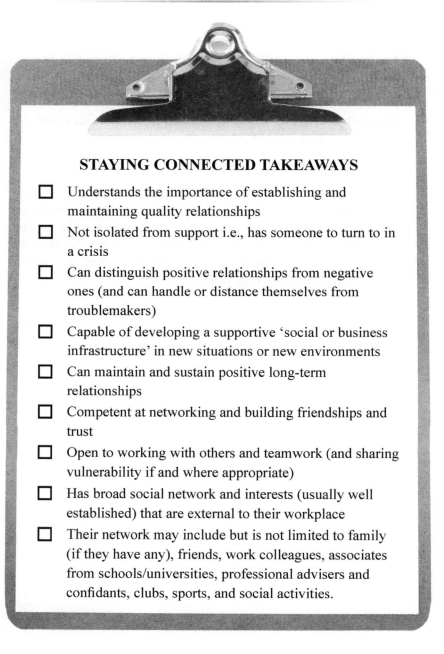

STAYING CONNECTED TAKEAWAYS

☐ Understands the importance of establishing and maintaining quality relationships

☐ Not isolated from support i.e., has someone to turn to in a crisis

☐ Can distinguish positive relationships from negative ones (and can handle or distance themselves from troublemakers)

☐ Capable of developing a supportive 'social or business infrastructure' in new situations or new environments

☐ Can maintain and sustain positive long-term relationships

☐ Competent at networking and building friendships and trust

☐ Open to working with others and teamwork (and sharing vulnerability if and where appropriate)

☐ Has broad social network and interests (usually well established) that are external to their workplace

☐ Their network may include but is not limited to family (if they have any), friends, work colleagues, associates from schools/universities, professional advisers and confidants, clubs, sports, and social activities.

Congratulations! You have reached the top of the Resilience Ladder. You should now have a greater understanding of how resilience works and how to apply the insights and principles in the 7 Steps to develop resilient responses and habits.

Becoming resilient is not something that will happen overnight. It is a continuously evolving process made up of incremental changes and purpose driven momentum, but even taking micro steps in the right direction is better than being stuck in negativity and anchored in denial. No one can do your heavy lifting for you. An investment of time, patience and dedication will be required to advance your objective and achieve a successful outcome and move forward.

You may like to record your progress in a journal or simply ask yourself "Where am I on the Resilience Ladder today?" If at any time you feel like you have lost your way and are 'falling off' your Resilience Ladder, understand that success is never measured by how many times you fall, only by how many times you rise. Get straight back up, but always start with Step 1 – Acceptance. Then use the other Steps and TakeAways to guide you back to a more positive, confident mindset, knowing that you are indeed on the pathway to developing lasting sustainable resilience.

If you accept and practise the 'TakeAways' contained in each step of the Resilience Ladder this will help you to grow in confidence that adjust to uncertainty, tackle change and challenges and face adversity head on.

PART IIII

THE CRANWELL-CAMBRIDGE RESILIENCE TEST™

GLOBAL PSYCHOMETRIC
— INSTITUTE —

THE CRANWELL-CAMBRIDGE RESILIENCE TEST™

THE STORY

What a difference a day makes…

Date: A Winter's day in early February 2020.

Time: Mid-morning.

Vehicle: Late model… black Mercedes S-Class.

Driver: Capped, uniformed and courteous. Believing that his passenger was a tourist out for a day trip, he was chatty and only too willing to provide commentary and point out landmarks to his captive audience believing that they were eager to hear his commentary. In that he was mistaken.

Passenger: The lady in the back seat stared blankly out the window but really saw nothing at all. Sightseeing was not on her mind. If anything, her face displayed a hint of apprehension.

Journey: The black limousine sped gracefully along the M11, the motorway that links London and Cambridge. As the vehicle approached its destination the driver said "Would Madam like to see the Bridge of Sighs, or The King's College Chapel? You know that this University is packed with historic buildings dating back centuries." "Thank you, maybe another day," was the quick reply, "but please wait in Trumpington Street, I'll be heading straight back to London... this shouldn't take more than an hour and a half."

A little crestfallen, he pulled up outside a relatively contemporary looking building on the Old Addenbrooke's Site, Trumpington Street, just a stone's throw from the world-renowned Fitzwilliam Museum. The GPS broke the silence: "You have now arrived at your destination. Your destination is on your left. You have now arrived at your destination. Your destination is on your left."

The Destination: *The air was crisp and bone-chilling cold as the passenger took her first step away from the warmth and safety of the car. She took a deep breath and made her way through the arched gateway entrance of the Cambridge Judge Business School at the University of Cambridge.*

The Meeting: *Between the Psychometrics Centre and the interested party.*

The Mission: *Reach an agreement acceptable to both parties.*

Her Strategy: *Appear confident and relaxed, listen carefully, stay open-minded and flexible but play to win.*

The Reality: *The stage was set. The stakes were high. Nerves relentlessly gnawed away at her self-belief. It seemed as if her whole life had come down to this moment. Failure was not an option.*

The Outcome: *Remarkably, the meeting which lasted over an hour seemed to fly by. Discussions went smoothly and were successful.*

The Adventure Begins!

And so began my collaboration with the Psychometrics Centre, to develop a test based on science and my theory and lived experience of resilience. The Psychometrics Centre, a world leader in the development of psychometric tests, commenced work on the Cranwell-Cambridge Resilience Test™ in mid-2020. By then the Covid-19 Pandemic had been declared and resilience skills seemed more essential than ever, but it wasn't the Pandemic that had triggered my thoughts about resilience.

The need for people with resilience skills

How to personally build and sustain resilience and had been on my mind ever since Richard's diagnosis of Younger Onset Alzheimer's in February 2003, but in late 2009 when he was admitted to a Secure Dementia Unit in an aged care facility, I started to think about resilience in aged care staff and in the workforce generally. I wondered if there was a way for employers to identify resilient people who could consistently cope better with challenging behaviours and sometimes stressful situations

The impact of staff changes and turnover on aged care residents

As a continuous visitor I closely observed Richard's interaction with his regular carers and the difference it made to his behaviour and habits when unfamiliar staff were looking after him. I became acutely aware of how unsettling staff changes and turnover were for him and the other residents. Continuity is very important to all residents in aged care, but especially those with memory loss who are struggling to hang on to some small measure of certainty in their daily lives. Of course, there will always be times when regular staff are rostered on to different shifts or they are sick or on leave. This is unavoidable, but the more that can be done to provide stability in the workforce, the better for all.

The revolving door

Richard spent five years in the Unit and during that time I observed many staff arrivals and departures. Unfortunately, some staff only lasted a few days while others had been there for years. It was easy enough to identify the long-timers. I watched Richard and the other residents' faces break out into beautiful smiles when they saw their favourite carers coming towards them and I also watched their confusion and how they struggled when new or unfamiliar carers or other staff entered the Unit.

Benefits of staff continuity and routine procedures

A huge advantage of having regular staff is the personal connection and knowledge of individual residents likes and dislikes when it comes to routine daily procedures like showering, dressing and eating. At one stage Richard's weight started to drop rapidly and we couldn't work out why. It wasn't until one of his regular carer's observed that his dementia had progressed to the extent that he had forgotten how to feed himself, that we discovered the cause of his weight loss. He was leaving most of his meals untouched because he was unable to co-ordinate his cognitive processes and motor actions to hold and use a knife and fork or even a spoon. Strategies were immediately put into place to see that he was supported during meal times and his weight quickly returned to normal.

The Cranwell Resilience Ladder™ and the Cranwell-Cambridge Resilience Test™

As the years that Richard was in care rolled by, I thought about resilience more and more and gradually the concept of the Cranwell Resilience Ladder ™ evolved to explain key resilience skills and principles in a simple, straightforward and easy-to-remember manner. Incorporating these learnings into a psychometric test supported by scientific research followed a few years later, resulting in the Cranwell-Cambridge Resilience Test™.

The Cranwell-Cambridge Resilience Test™ : Purpose and Scope

The purpose of the test is to accurately assess a candidate's level of resilience by scientifically measuring their ability to cope with situations that may involve frequent change and disruption, ongoing and increasing uncertainty and mild to significant adversity. Unlike some other psychometric tests, the scope of the Cranwell-Cambridge Resilience Test™ is intentionally broad. It is not limited to occupation type, seniority rank or specific industries. The Test is suitable for entry level to executive candidates because it is designed specifically to look closely at the person, i.e., to 'drill down' into the individual's unique personality and provide valuable insights that are not easily identifiable by other means.

Key features

Some key features of the Cranwell-Cambridge Resilience Test™ include:

- Unique online tool

- Scientifically based

- Reliability

- Validity

- Objectivity: minimises the risk of bias for prospective employees

- Norm-referenced

- User friendly online format

- Rapid results

- Mobile device friendly, and

- Takes approximately 10 – 15 minutes

Use: recruitment and professional development

Prospective candidates may be invited to undertake the test by an employer or recruitment agency very early in the recruitment process, while others may choose to assess candidates further before requiring them to undertake the test. Use of the test need not be limited to external recruitment. Internal assessment opportunities may include assessing staff for new positions, restructuring, internal promotions, improving retention rates, identifying future executives and team leaders, professional development initiatives, mental health and well-being programs or cultural change. The test may also provide useful insights for franchisors looking to screen potential franchisees.

Use: individual self-knowledge

Alternatively, an individual may opt to take the test because they are curious about their ability to undertake a new challenge or career change and wish to better inform themselves about their level of resilience. Obtaining this personal knowledge may help provide them with guidance towards future job and lifestyle opportunities. Proactive job seekers may also like to provide their results from the Cranwell-Cambridge Resilience Test ™ in their job application along with their cover letter, CV or resume.

Businesses and industries

There are many types of businesses and Industries that may benefit from the Cranwell-Cambridge Resilience Test™. These include but are not limited to:

- Aged Care
- Physical Health, Mental Health & Wellbeing
- Emergency Services (Police, Fire, Ambulance)

- Defence Forces
- Sales
- Security
- Franchising
- Community & Social Services
- Government Departments (Federal, State, Local)
- Tertiary Institutions, Training Institutions, Education (Primary and Secondary) & Technical Schools
- Insurance, Accounting, Superannuation, Banking, Finance & Legal
- Forestry, Fisheries, Agriculture, Primary Producers
- Mining, Resources & Energy
- Consulting, Human Resources, Administration & Recruitment
- Small Business
- Engineering & Manufacturing
- Veterinary Services
- Information & Communication Technology
- Trades & Services
- Viticulture
- Advertising & Media
- Real Estate Sales & Property Development
- Building & Construction
- Arts, Entertainment & Events
- Tourism, Accommodation & Hospitality
- Sports & Recreation
- Weddings & Funerals
- Retail, Sales & Services
- Prison Services
- Transport & Logistics

For those seeking more information about the Cranwell-Cambridge Resilience Test™ you can find it at:

www.GlobalPsychometricInstitute.com

The Cranwell-Cambridge Resilience Test™

APPENDIX I

BUSINESS CRISIS GUIDANCE FAST TRACK

What keeps you awake at night?

Identify, analyse and focus on your worst-case scenarios and plan for them. In a crisis it's far easier to scale down your response if the situation turns out to be manageable, than to scale up if you are not prepared. Remember, the element of surprise works well in a chess game when you are on the attack but falls dangerously short when your response to a crisis is limited by lack of foresight and preparation.

Don't get caught with your pants down

Survival of the fittest now belongs to the agile, those who foresee the storm clouds coming and take fast strategic action. Learning to expect and prepare for the unexpected will help protect you and your business from threats to your reputation, operations, people, assets and finances and minimise harmful effects.

Hope is NOT a strategy

Develop a Crisis Management Strategy and Plan. Businesses and organisations that lack sustainable resilience strategies and robust resilient leaders and employees risk languishing behind their competitors and setting themselves up for Darwinian-style extinction.

Does size matter?

No, not in this context. Safety, security and survival are not the exclusive prerogative of the corporate elite. Whether you are a sole operator or your business is a small family business, small to medium company, large corporation or government department, the size of the business does not alter the importance of having good up-to-date crisis management and business continuity plans. Even a very small business can have a one-to-two-page plan and an up-to-date list of their essential emergency contacts.

Resilient leadership

Have a strong resilient leadership team to lead and guide your staff to implement your crisis plan and steer the business to recovery and beyond. Remember, not everyone in your business or organisation is cut out to be a leader or assist the leadership during a crisis. Just because someone is a subject matter expert or has 'manager' or 'executive' somewhere in their title or job description does not automatically make them the best person to handle crisis situations. You need people who are capable of following and implementing your crisis plan, but if necessary they are also capable of using their initiative and will not mentally 'freeze' under the stress and uncertainty of the situation.

Crisis plans

Keep your plans clear, simple and easy to read so that anyone in the business or organisation can read and understand them, especially when they are stressed and under pressure. No one has time to read a tome in a crisis! No matter how good they look, large volumes of expensive glossy crisis response and management plans may be counter-productive in a crisis. Lengthy complicated plans may actually impede response, restoration of essential services and long-term business continuity.

Where to start?

Start with conducting a business risk assessment to identify and prioritise your key risks. Conduct a business impact analysis. Take steps to mitigate your risks. Determine the scope of the plan and always plan for the worst-case scenario. Clarify roles and responsibilities so that everyone knows exactly what they must do. Ensure the plan distinguishes between what needs to be done urgently and what can wait.

Scale and triage

Ensure your plan identifies your highest to lowest priorities and is scalable. Your plan must include surge capacity i.e., the ability to escalate rapidly from zero to a full-scale crisis. Also include a triage criterion and a process capable of assessing the appropriate degree of urgency to address personnel and business key priorities in a crisis.

Review, update and practice plans regularly

Review and update your crisis plan on a scheduled basis, say every 12 or 24 months and update after every incident or crisis. Provide staff training and test run the plan so that all staff and management know how it operates and where they fit in. Everyone needs to feel confident in their role and know exactly what is expected of them. Exercises and drills should be conducted regularly so that when an incident occurs people are prepared and go about their crisis roles automatically without needing prompting.

How long is a piece of string?

The duration of a crisis is another factor which is critical to consider when writing crisis plans. How far out does your response extend? Is it sustainable? Can your response last three months, six months, twelve months or be ongoing without your business collapsing?

Business continuity

Examine the interdependencies between key business areas and critical functions. Calculate the downtime for each identified critical function and the implications if the downtime is excessive. Minimise or temporarily suspend any nonessential services. Develop strategic actions to keep essential and priority services operating. You may want to consider whether to discontinue some nonessential services permanently or for the time being and focus on the currently more profitable or essential ones.

What happens 'when the music stops'?

Always conduct a post-exercise, post-incident or post-crisis review.

Evaluate the lessons learned:

- What worked well?
- What went wrong?
- What could we do better next time?
- How could we do it better next time?

APPENDIX II (a)

CRISIS MANAGEMENT PLAN CHECKLIST

FOR MEDIUM TO LARGE BUSINESS

The purpose of this list is for general guidance only, it is not exhaustive. You may wish to consider including these key components in your Crisis Management Plan and/or adding more checkpoints that are unique to your business.

Depending on the size of your business and the estimated scale and potential duration of the crisis you may wish to develop separate and more detailed plans for specific situations e.g., Pandemic, Media, Major Disaster Recovery, Security and Business Continuity.

FOR MEDIUM TO LARGE BUSINESS

Tick	Crisis Plan Checklist
	Date of Plan and Review Date
	Include a Risks Assessment in which you identify and prioritise Hazards (Threats), Risk Likelihood and Mitigation Measures.
	Scope and Application ***Typical external business hazards may include but are not limited to:*** Public Health, Pandemic, Cyberattack, Power Failure, Network Outage, Flood, Drought, Fire, Legal, Regulatory Compliance, Natural Disasters, Climate Change, Terrorist Incident, Political, Economic Sanctions, Supply Chain Failure, Reputational Damage, Liability, Biosecurity, Foreign Exchange Rates, Competition, Artificial Intelligence, Digital Divide. ***Typical internal business threats may include but are not limited to:*** Financial (i.e., strategic decisions and cashflow), Data Loss, Insider Threat (i.e., disgruntled employee), Staff Retention, Confidential Information Loss, Operational (i.e., property and assets damage or failure), Criminal Activity or Fraud, Security, Inadequate Communication and Transparency Between Business Areas, Negative Workplace Practices and Culture, Inadequate Physical Safety and/or Health and Mental Wellbeing Safety Nets
	Mitigation measures may include but are not limited to: Risk Transfer or Outsourcing, Data Backup and Analytics Tools, Cloud Storage Systems, Automation, Off-site Facilities and Capabilities, Cyber and Physical Security, Employee Risk-Management Education, Personnel Security, Safety, Health and Mental Health Measures

FOR MEDIUM TO LARGE BUSINESS

Tick	Crisis Plan Checklist
	List your Crisis Contacts e.g., Up-to-the-moment contacts for Police, Emergency Services, Public Health, Telecommunications, Security, Internet Provider, Power, Water, Gas and Electricity Service Providers, Insurance, IT security, Landlord (if applicable), Bank, Accountant, Clients, Suppliers, Neighbouring Businesses, Government, Media and Industry
	Arrange a designated location for Crisis Command Centre (if appropriate)
	Identify Key Crisis Response and Management Roles, Responsibilities, Contact Details
	Identify Essential Services Priorities, Business Continuity Arrangements for moving forward
	Security Arrangements
	Establish Evacuation Procedures and include Building/Site Exit Map
	Develop Lockdown Actions
	Covid Safety Procedures: Protective Physical Equipment and Measures e.g., Masks, Hand Sanitisers, Gloves, Covid Safe Check-In Procedures and Signs, Covid Safe Staff Training, Social Distancing Measures, Covid Marshalls etc.
	Media and Social Media Arrangements
	Review and Audit Schedule, Responsibilities and Arrangements
	Incident Log, Recording and Reporting Arrangements
	Staff Training and Drills Schedule
	Analysis of 'Lessons Learned' from drills or incidents
	Crisis Plan Activation Date and Authorisation Signature ....
	Checklist Completed (insert date) ....

APPENDIX II (b)

CRISIS MANAGEMENT PLAN TEMPLATE

FOR MEDIUM TO LARGE BUSINESS

DATE & REVIEW DATE:		
BUSINESS RISK ASSESSMENT:		
SCOPE & APPLICATION:		

Crisis Contacts	Name	Phone number
Emergency Services	Fire/police/ ambulance	000
Police		
Public Health	Covid Information	
Key Managers & Staff		
Security		
Power		
Water		
Gas		
Internet		
Telecommunications		
IT, IT Security		
Landlord		

FOR MEDIUM TO LARGE BUSINESS

Crisis Contacts	Name	Phone number
Bank		
Media		
Accountant		
Clients		
Suppliers		
Insurance		
Business Neighbours		
Industry		
Government		
Crisis Command Centre Activation:		
Key Crisis Roles & Responsibilities:		
Essential Services Priorties, Business Continuity:		
Security Arrangements		
Evacuation Procedures & Exit Map:		
Lockdown Procedures:		
Media Arrangements:		
Covid-19 Procedures:		
Review & Audit Schedule, Responsibilities & Arrangements:		
Incident Recording Log, Recording & Reporting Arrangements:		
Staff Crisis Training & Drill Schedule:		
Analysis From Drills & Incidents:		

FOR MEDIUM TO LARGE BUSINESS

Links To Detailed Plans:	
• Pandemic • Media • Security • Major Disaster • Business Continuity	
Authorisation & Signature:	

APPENDIX III (a)

CRISIS MANAGEMENT PLAN CHECKLIST

FOR SMALL BUSINESS OR SOLE PROPRIETOR

In the case of a small business owner or sole proprietor there is often no one to delegate the task of writing the Crisis Management Plan to because 'the buck stops with you'. Don't let that deter you. No one knows your business better than you do. Keep your plan clear, short and simple. A one to two A4 size page is better than no plan at all. If you do have staff, ensure the plan is made known to all (permanent fulltime, part-time and casuals) and kept in a secure but accessible location and keep a duplicate copy elsewhere.

The purpose of this list is for general guidance purposes only and it is not exhaustive. You may wish to consider using these key components in your Crisis Management Plan or using this list as a base for adding more checkpoints to your plan that are unique to your business.

FOR SMALL BUSINESS OR SOLE PROPRIETOR

Tick	Crisis Plan Checklist
	Date of Plan and Review Date…………..
	Include a Risk Assessment in which you identify and prioritise Hazards (threats), Risk Likelihood and Mitigation (i.e., prevention/protective) Measures
	Scope and Application *Typical external business hazards may include but are not limited to:* Public Health and Pandemic, Cyberattack, Power Failure, Network Outage, Flood, Drought, Fire, Legal, Regulatory Compliance, Natural Disasters, Climate Change, Terrorist Incident, Political, Economic Sanctions, Supply Chain Failure, Reputational Damage, Liability, Foreign Exchange Rates, Competition, Artificial Intelligence *Typical internal threats for small business or sole proprietors may include but are not limited to:* Financial (i.e., strategic decisions and cashflow), Insider Threat (i.e., disgruntled employee), Staff Retention, Owner/Manager or Essential Staff Injury, Prolonged Illness or Death, Operational (i.e., property and assets damage or failure), Criminal Activity or Fraud, Security, Physical and Mental Safety and Wellbeing, Inadequate Insurance, Inadequate Succession Planning
	Mitigation Measures that prevent or minimise loss or damage may include but are not limited to: Outsourcing, Data Backup, Analytical Tools, Cloud Storage Systems, Mobile Electronic Capability and Video Conferencing Facilities, Cyber Security, Physical Security (e.g., CCTV), Staff Health, Safety and Wellbeing Measures, Insurance for worst case scenario, Pre-emptive Succession Planning

FOR SMALL BUSINESS OR SOLE PROPRIETOR

Tick	Crisis Plan Checklist
	List your Crisis Contacts e.g., Up-to-the-moment contacts for Police, Emergency Services, Public Health, Telecommunications, Internet Provider, Power, Water, Gas and Electricity Service Providers, Insurance, IT security, Landlord (if applicable), Bank, Clients, Suppliers, Neighbouring Businesses, Media, Government, Industry and Staff Contacts
	Identify Key Crisis Response and Management Roles and Responsibilities (if you have staff)
	Security Arrangements
	Establish Evacuation Procedures and include Building/Site Exit Map
	Develop Lockdown Actions
	Identify Essential Services Priorities and Business Continuity Arrangements for moving forward
	Covid-19 Safety Procedures (as appropriate) e.g., Masks, Hand Sanitisers, Gloves, Covid Safe Check-In, Covid Safe Social Distancing, Signage etc.
	Incident Management Recording Log
	Crisis Response Training and Drills Schedule (if you have staff)
	Analysis of 'Lessons Learned' from drills or incidents (if applicable)
	Review and Update Plan Schedule
	Crisis Plan Activation Date and Authorisation Signature ....
	Checklist Completed (insert date)

APPENDIX III (b)

CRISIS MANAGEMENT PLAN TEMPLATE FOR SMALL BUSINESS OR SOLE PROPRIETOR

DATE & REVIEW DATE:		
BUSINESS RISK ASSESSMENT:		
SCOPE & APPLICATION:		

Crisis Contacts	Name	Phone number
Emergency Services	Fire/police/ ambulance	000
Police		
Public Health	Covid Information	
Designated Managers/Staff		
Power		
Water		
Gas		
Internet		
Telecommunications		
IT, IT Security		

FOR SMALL BUSINESS OR SOLE PROPRIETOR

Crisis Contacts	Name	Phone number
Landlord		
Bank		
Accountant		
Clients		
Suppliers		
Insurance		
Government, Industry, Business Neighbours		
Staff & Temporary Staff		
Crisis Roles & Responsibilities:		
Evacuation Procedures & Exit Map:		
Covid-19 Procedures:		
Lockdown Procedures:		
Incident Recording Log		
Crisis Training & Drills:		
Review & Audit Schedule:		
Lessons Learned From Drills/ Incidents:		
Authorisation / Signature:		

ABOUT THE AUTHOR

CAROLYN CRANWELL LLB GDLP

 Carolyn is an Author, Resilience Coach, Founder and Executive Director of the Global Psychometric Institute, Speaker and qualified lawyer. Her professional career spanned nearly 20 years in government in various ministerial and public service roles including providing strategic policy advice to State Government Ministers and Chief Executives. The greater part of Carolyn's career was spent as a Senior Adviser on counter-terrorism and emergency management for the public transport system in South Australia.

Married to Richard Cranwell for 32 years, Carolyn was his primary carer for 18 of those years after he developed Younger Onset Alzheimer's. At the time of diagnosis Richard owned and operated a retail business in a large coastal shopping centre. Carolyn had a busy full-time job and they had two school age children. It was primarily during this challenging and often stressful period that she honed her personal resilience skills. Carolyn learnt how to draw on her previously largely untapped emotional and mental strength. This experience became the key stone of her concept known as the Cranwell Resilience Ladder™ featured in *Hardcore Resilience – Seven Steps to Building Successful and Lasting Resilience in Your Business and Your Life* and guided the criteria for the Cranwell-Cambridge Resilience Test™, a psychometric test Carolyn developed collaboratively with The Psychometrics Centre, University of Cambridge.

Carolyn lives near the inner city and parklands in Adelaide, South Australia. She is a frequent traveller and loves visiting her adult son, daughter, son-in-law and grandchildren who all live in the United Kingdom.

Carolyn is the author of:

- *Navigating Alzheimer's – Survival Secrets of a Long Term Carer*
- Hardcore Resilience – Seven Steps to Building Successful and Lasting Resilience in Your Business and Your Life

Other work includes:

- The *Cranwell-Cambridge Resilience Test* ™, in collaboration with The Psychometrics Centre, University of Cambridge, UK
- Founder and Executive Director of the Global Psychometric Institute

Website:
www.GlobalPsychometricInstitute.com

RECOMMENDED RESOURCES

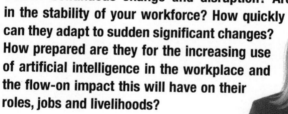

PRESENTATION FORMATS

▶ **Workshops**

These workshops are suitable for larger groups and consist of a program tailored to your business or organisation's needs. Participants will be guided on how to navigate the seven step Cranwell Resilience Ladder ™, and how to develop and implement their personal resilience plan.

Workshops include a copy of Hardcore Resilience – *7 Steps to Building Successful and Lasting Resilience in Your Business and Your Life, a Cranwell Resilience Ladder™ Workbook and a Personal Resilience Journal.*

▶ **Small Groups and One-on-One Coaching**

I will work personally with teams and individuals to address any specific areas of concern.

▶ **Custom Programs and Packages**

Custom Programs and Packages can be tailored to your business and employees' needs.

▶ **Speaking Events**

We can provide an engaging and thought provoking talk that will leave your conference or meeting participants with a new appreciation for the critical importance of a positive attitude for themselves and their team, and the mental health and wellbeing benefits from practicing and mastering resilience skills.

▶ **Cranwell-Cambridge Resilience Test™**

To get the maximum benefit from Workshops or Coaching sessions all participants will be invited to undertake the online Cranwell-Cambridge Resilience Test™ prior to commencement. Results will be provided to participants on a confidential basis.

Enquiries to www.GlobalPsychometricInstitute.com

Discover How Resilient You Are!

Why not take the world leading Resilience test designed to discover and accurately assess your level of resilience by scientifically measuring your ability to cope with situations that may involve frequent change and disruption, ongoing and increasing uncertainty and mild to significant adversity. Find your hidden strengths today!

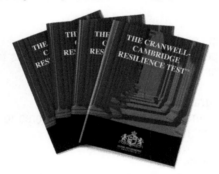

The Cranwell-Cambridge Resilience Test™
Go to this link right NOW!
www.GlobalPsychometricInstitute.com/test

GLOBAL PSYCHOMETRIC
— INSTITUTE —

BONUS GIFT

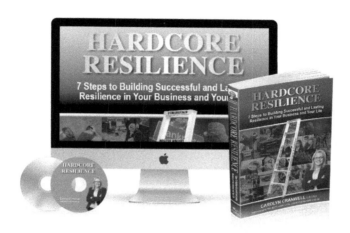

Claim your BONUS GIFTS by going to
www.HardcoreResilience.com/Bonus-Gifts

Instant Access and FREE Download

We can't give you everything you need to know about Resilience in one small book.

So, we've created a very special website with extra resources just for you. You'll find crisis plans, checklists and templates.

Carolyn

Claim your BONUS GIFTS by going to
www.HardcoreResilience.com/Bonus-Gifts

NOTES

1. Gemma Aburn, Merryn Gott and Karen Hoare, 'Review of the Empirical Literature', *Journal of Advanced Nursing*, Jan 2016, NZ.

2. Jim Rohn, American author and entrepreneur noted for his motivational sayings.

3. Charles Dickens, opening page, *A Tale of Two Cities,* serialised in All Year Rounder, London, 1859.

4. C. William Pollard, American business leader and author.

5. J.K Rowling, *Very Good Lives: The Fringe Benefits of Failure and the Importance of Imagination*, speech, Harvard Commencement Space, research from Goodreads & Google.

6. Lewis Carroll, *Alice's Adventures in Wonderland*, London, 1865.

7. Spanish Flu history research Wikipedia

8. Viktor Frankl, *Man's Search for Meaning*, first published Germany 1946, UK Random House.

9. Ibid.

10. Hamish McLachlan, *Herald Sun*, Melbourne, Nov 7, 2015.

11. One to one interview, *Source Kids*, Nov 26, 2018.

12. Diane Contu in *Harvard Business Review*, May 2002 in reference to Jim Collins *Good to Great* Oct 16, 2001.

13. S. Cheney & D. Richards *Australian Story* ABC TV, May 2020.

14. Alexandra Smith, *Sydney Morning Herald*, April 6, 2020.

15. ABC TV News, March 26, 2021.

16. Kellogg history research Wikipedia.

17. James Surowicki, 'Hanging Tough', *New Yorker*, April 4, 2009.

18. Allen Saunders, *Readers Digest*, Jan 1957. Popularised in 'Beautiful Boy' by John Lennon, 1980.

19. Traci Tong, Napalm Girl Public Radio International, Feb 21, 2018.

20. Don DeLillo, *White Noise*, Viking Press, USA.

21. Janine Allis, *The Accidental Entrepreneur*, Wiley, Qld, 2016.

22. M. Bailey, *Australian Financial Review*, Syd, Nov 11, 2019.

23. Ricardo Goncalves, SBS News, Oct 24, 2019.

24. Ibid.

25. D Coleman, *Emotional Intelligence* Focus- The Hidden Driver of Excellence, USA, 1995.

26. Caleb Bush, *CEO Magazine*, USA, 2019.

27. Russell Telford, from A G Coombs.

28. D. Robertson & B. Breen, *Brick by Brick*, Penguin, June 2013.

29. Ibid.

30. Nick Craig *Leading from Purpose*, pub by the author, June 2018.

31. Albert Einstein, comments on Purpose

32. Joshua Robertson, *Guardian*, Jan 2017.

33. *Our Community Leaders-Great Australian Leaders in Focus*, ourCommunity.com.au, Melbourne, Oct 2010.

34. Viktor Frankl, Op. Cit.

35. Sara Blakely history research Wikipedia

36. Inc 5000, The 2020 List, inc.com.

37. Anthony, Trotter & Schwartz, 'The Top 20 Business Transformations of the Last Decade', *Harvard Business Review*, Sept 24, 2019.

38. Biography.com Editors, *Malala Yousafzai Biography*, Biography.com, Mar 29, 2018

39. Widely attributed to Albert Einstein, Stephen Hawking added, "Adapt to change."

40. Charlie Munger, in speech to Harvard School, quoting Jacobi, June 1986.

41. ABC News, June 3, 2020.

42. *The Advertiser*, Adelaide Now, Oct 11, 2020.

43. Info from homepage, www.stagekings.com.au

44. James Collins and Jerry Porras, *Built to Last*, Harper Collins, NY 1994.

45. Wikipedia quoting from *Wall Street Journal* & *Star Tribune* USA Mar, 2021.

46. Matt Clarkson and Amanda Clarkson, *100 Magic Tips for eBay*, Global Publishing Group, Melbourne, 2011.

47. Norman Vincent Pearl, *The Power of Positive Thinking*, Prentice Hall, USA, 1952.

48. Roger Federer, widely quoted 2018.

49. Alexis Teasdale, *The Happiness Tonic We Need in 2020*, Kiddomag.com.au Oct/Dec 2020.

50. *Sydney Morning Herald*, Feb 23, 2017.

51. Info from Starbucks homepage & Wikipedia

52. Calvin Coolidge, 30th President of the USA.

53. Jack Canfield and Janet Switze, *The Success Principles,* Dec 28, 2004.

54. Jack Canfield, Mark Victor Hansen and Sharon J. Wohlmuth, *Chicken Soup for the Soul* book series in the 1990s HCL Florida.

55. Ken Blanchard, motivational writer most noted for *The One-Minute Manager.*

56. Sir James Dyson interviewed for Fast Company magazine, May 2007.

57. Historical research from Wikipedia.

58. Walter Mischel, *The Marshmallow Test*, Transworld, London 2014

59. J K Rowling history from Wikipedia.

60. J K Rowling, *Harry Potter* series: seven volumes and films, Bloomsbury, London 1997–2007

61. John Donne, 'No Man is an Island', London 1624.

62. ABC News Oct 12, 2020.

63. Abbie Wightman, *The South Wales police officer who helped track down Europe's notorious war criminals*, Wales Online, May 31, 2015.

64. Howard Tucker, correspondence with the author, March 25, 2021.

65. R Jay Turner, *Social Support as a contingency in psychological well-being*, Journal of Health & Social Behaviour, USA, 1981.

*Carolyn Cranwell, *Navigating Alzheimer's – Survival Secrets of a Long Term Carer*, Global Publishing Group, Melbourne, 2016

Printed in Australia
AUHW010135230123
373712AU00015B/15